PRAIS[E FOR]

Return [to Life]

Return to Life is literally like 10 d[...] Pam Butler writes from the heart and offers healing calm and soothing balms for the soul in every passage. Read this book and feel your stress dissolve and your soul soar!

– Rudolph E. Tanzi, Ph.D.,
Author of *The Healing Self, Super Brain* and *Super Genes*

Return to Life is a powerful reminder that no matter how hard life gets, we can fully transform and enjoy a whole, balanced and happy life. Pam Butler shares the raw details of her life's dramatic highs and lows and her powerful journey to wellness and loving herself.

– Tara Stiles,
founder of Strala Yoga

Return to Life is a beautiful and essential resource for anyone who has experienced hardship or trauma, from depression, anxiety and PTSD to divorce, illness and loss. By offering up her personal stories along with simple, powerful techniques for finding peace, Pam shows that no matter what happens, you can live a life full of bliss.

– Gabrielle Bernstein,
#1 *New York Times* Bestselling Author

Pam Butler's extraordinary book is like a balm for anyone and everyone who has experienced loss, pain, extreme life challenges, or is simply challenged by daily stress. Filled with wisdom, insights, and immensely practical strategies, the practices and suggestions that Pam teaches are helpful for anyone who feels the need to rebalance themselves, and find strength, stability and happiness again in their lives. As Pam shares her heroic journey of self-discovery in this book, she, at the same time, gives us the tools to discover our own Self.

– Eddie Stern,
Ashtanga Yoga Teacher, Co-founder of Ashtanga
Yoga New York, the Brooklyn Club

Pam Butler has been a longtime friend of The Chopra Foundation who has embraced meditation and yoga to transform her life to be able to help others.

– Deepak Chopra,
Author of *The Healing Self*

Return to Life

Finding Your Way Back to Balance and Bliss in a Stressed-Out World

PAM BUTLER

HAY HOUSE

Published in Australia by: Hay House Australia Pty. Ltd.: www.hayhouse.com.au
Published in the United States by: Hay House, Inc.: www.hayhouse.com
Published in the United Kingdom by: Hay House UK, Ltd.: www.hayhouse.co.uk
Published in India by: Hay House Publishers India: www.hayhouse.co.in

Design by Rhett Nacson
Typeset by Bookhouse, Sydney

ISBN: 9781401950835
Digital ISBN: 9781401950910

21 20 19 18 4 3 2 1
1st edition, May 2018

Printed in Australia by McPherson's Printing Group

Dedication

To Brittany, my source of inspiration and strength—
Thank you for all the laughter and love
you have brought into my life

To the memory of my dad, who encouraged me no matter what
and believed in me always—I miss you

Contents

A Note to the Reader

If you've found your way to this book, it's probably because you've experienced some hard times in your life. Maybe you've lived through a breakup or an illness; the death of someone close to you; or a period of high stress, anxiety, or debilitating depression. Maybe you've experienced all of the above at once. If you've ever experienced the kind of brought-you-to-your-knees moments that I'm talking about, this book has been written with you in mind. My hope is that it can serve as a kind of guide for finding your way back from the brink, a place you can turn to for the advice, tools, information, and inspiration you need to get through it … and more.

Return to Life grew out of my own fifteen-plus year journey encompassing illness, divorce, the deaths of people close to me, the near-deaths of some others, recurring periods of depression, lots of stress and anxiety, and even a PTSD diagnosis (more on all that in the coming chapters). These were hard times, but I am happy to say that I didn't just survive them; I overcame them and thrived.

Since those dark days many years ago, I have become an inspirational speaker, a certified meditation and yoga teacher, and a bliss coach who uses a unique combination of body movement and mind practices to help people examine their responses to stress and learn techniques to shift into a state of balance, well-being, and ultimately, bliss. But this is not a book about me. It's really a book about you. Everyone has his or her own story to tell. Some stories are more traumatic than others, and some people may even think that what I went through pales in comparison to their own experiences. They may even be right, but the larger truth is that there isn't a person on this planet who hasn't faced hardship. None of us is alone in this. We all know that life can be messy, complicated, heartbreaking, and worse. But what I believe is also true is that the darkest of times provide some of the best opportunities for light, opportunities to learn, grow, and change our lives for the better. As the great mythologist Joseph Campbell once wrote, "It is by going down into the abyss that we recover the treasures of life."

When we're young, we're taught how to walk and talk, read and write, but we aren't taught what to do when life feels insurmountable. That is ultimately why I wrote this book. Many years ago when I was feeling lost and didn't know where to turn, this is the book I wish I had been able to find in my local bookstore to help me feel less alone and provide me with some guidance on how to make things better. This insights and tools in this book helped me "return to life," and I hope they can do the same for you.

Before I went on my own journey, I had no particular expertise in transforming my life or living in bliss. But after a long and winding road, I found these things were possible for me, and the result has been a much more peaceful, much more purposeful, much happier life that I wouldn't trade for anything. If it's possible for me, then it's possible for you! Whatever life brings, you deserve to live in bliss. So let's get started!

CHAPTER ONE

Lost and Alone

"Even when you think you have your life all mapped out, things happen that shape your destiny in ways you might never even have imagined."

—Deepak Chopra

She's dead! I was sure of it. When my baby girl was finally born, she wasn't crying. She wasn't screaming. She made no sound at all. And no sound was the worst sound I'd ever heard in my life.

I caught my first glimpse of her as they whisked her away from me and deposited her pale, unmoving body on a table next to me. They started working on her immediately, their movements swift and precise. She wasn't breathing, so they suctioned fluid from her air passage. Her heartbeat was faint, so they pressed down on her tiny frame to perform chest compressions. A breathing tube was inserted in her throat so they could hook her up to a ventilator. It was all happening so quickly. And so silently. All I could hear was the mechanical beeping and clanking of medical equipment. All I could do was watch and wonder if my newborn baby was dying in front of me. Or, if she was already dead, and they just weren't telling me yet.

How had this happened? It felt just like moments before, when my doctor told me I was suffering from preeclampsia, a condition that could be life threatening for both me and my baby. It meant that the baby needed to come out—now. But that was okay. We'd known this could happen. She'd been given steroid injections in utero to hasten her lung development, just in case. It was still three weeks before her due date, but that wasn't so very long. Everything should have been fine. It should have been.

The doctor induced labor, and then we waited. I opted for a vaginal birth, and even with the drugs I'd been given to speed things along, it took hours. It had been about 4:00 a.m. when the doctor told me what we needed to do. It was the middle of the afternoon by the time the baby, whom we planned to name Brittany, entered the birth canal. And that was when all hell broke loose.

The baby suddenly stopped breathing. She stopped breathing, and they couldn't get her out. A level-three neonatal unit was called, and doctors stood on chairs on either side of me, pressing hard on my stomach over and over again, trying to force her free. My husband, Steve, stood behind me, bracing my head so I could push. But it wasn't working. Brittany wasn't breathing, and she wouldn't budge.

So they performed an emergency episiotomy, cutting me vaginally from front to back to get her out. When the baby finally arrived, you could have heard a pin drop in the room.

No one wanted to say anything because there was nothing good to say. Once she was out, and the neonatal team took over, I was hoping for some reassurance from my own doctor, but she was slumped over the delivery table holding her head in her hands instead. One look at Brittany's sheet-white form and everyone in the room—my doctor, the nurses, the neonatal team, Steve, and even me in my state of near-delirium—knew instantly just how bad things really were.

The hours that had passed to get us to this moment felt like they'd gone by in an instant. But now, every moment they worked on Brittany felt like forever. As the seconds dragged into minutes with still no one explaining what was happening, I became even more certain that she wasn't going to make it. Then all of a sudden, without a word, the neonatal team gathered up my daughter and rushed her toward the door. In the split second before exiting the room, one of them paused and said to me, "Do you want to see her?" Of course I wanted to see her, of course I did, but I couldn't think, I couldn't speak. I just lay there staring at them blankly, so they turned away and wheeled Brittany out the door.

As I watched them go, I wanted to cry out. I wanted scream at them to tell me something, anything at all. I wanted to get up out of my bed and run after Brittany, to hold her, to follow them wherever they were going, but I couldn't. They had beaten me up pretty good while trying to get her out. And just a few seconds later, it suddenly became clear that something was very wrong with me as well.

With Brittany out of the room, attention turned back to me still lying there on the delivery table. That was when someone realized that I hadn't delivered the placenta. Once again, there were doctors and nurses on either side of me pushing on my stomach, trying to get the placenta to come out before it turned toxic. As they pushed and pushed, something finally gave way, but it wasn't the placenta. I started hemorrhaging blood.

It took more than an hour before they were able to stop the bleeding and stitch me up. Afterward, I was taken to intensive care, where all I could do was lie there and wait. Someone encouraged me to get some rest, as if that were possible. I still hadn't heard a thing about Brittany, and my mind was spinning. I couldn't believe this was actually happening. In a perfect world, nurses were supposed to clean up my daughter and present her to my husband and me in a cute little bundle, all pink and squawking. Then our families were supposed to appear to congratulate us on what a beautiful family we were.

Instead, I was lying in bed, with no baby and no visitors, wondering what would happen to us. It had taken me so long to get to this place, and I couldn't believe it might all end like this. I'd always dreamed of becoming a mom, and it had already been a difficult road. My first pregnancy had ended in a miscarriage, after which I went through multiple fertility treatments to get pregnant again with Brittany. I'd been so careful this time around, doing everything I could not to lose another baby. I went to get an ultrasound as often as they'd let me. I even purchased a monitor so I could check her heartbeat at home. I watched what I ate and exercised regularly. I made sure not to risk a thing.

I'd done everything right, and look what had happened. At that very moment, I had no idea if either one of us was going to live or die.

This was definitely not how I'd pictured my life.

Out of the Frying Pan and into the Fire

You've undoubtedly experienced moments in your life when a traumatic event came crashing down out of nowhere, breaking the comfortable order of your life into a million jagged little pieces. Maybe the company you were working for got sold or taken over and you lost your job overnight. Maybe you found out that your partner was cheating on you and your relationship was finished all at once. Maybe you went to the doctor and got a dreaded medical diagnosis that changed everything. Often it isn't the traumatic moment itself that's the most difficult to handle. It's the aftermath, when you don't know what to do, what will come next, or how you will ever be able to put the pieces of your life back together again. That's what was happening to me following the birth of my daughter, which was supposed to be the happiest moment of my life.

Brittany was born on July 28, 1997, at four in the afternoon. It wasn't until about seven that evening when the neonatal doctor finally came to tell me what was happening with her. When they'd rushed her from the delivery room, they'd taken her to neonatal intensive care, where she'd received a blood transfusion. She was stable for now, but the outlook wasn't good. The doctor told me that during delivery, Brittany had been deprived of oxygen for approximately eight minutes. We would have to wait and see if that had resulted in any brain damage. They also weren't sure what had caused the need for a blood transfusion or if she would need another. Again, the best the doctor could offer was, "We'll have to wait and see."

After the doctor left, Steve visited Brittany in the NICU, but I wasn't allowed to go. I wasn't in any shape to leave my bed, so the nurses very kindly took Polaroid pictures of Brittany to show to me, and took pictures of me and Steve to tape to her incubator. That gave me a small measure of comfort, but mostly I was just living hour by hour. In the days that followed, it seemed like I was always waiting for some kind of news. *Would she need another blood transfusion?* No, it turned out, that wasn't going to be necessary. *Would she be able to breathe on her own once they took her off the ventilator?* Yes, miraculously she was able to breathe on her own. *Would she be able to eat once they removed her feeding tube?* I desperately wanted to breastfeed my baby once they took out the tube, but I couldn't, given that I was on bed rest and she was in an incubator in the NICU. So I pumped breast milk that the nurses bottle-fed to her. And Brittany did, in fact, eat. These were all promising signs.

It wasn't until two days after her birth that I was able to hold my baby for the first time. The day after that, the doctors declared me well enough to leave intensive care and move up to maternity. I couldn't stay in the same room as Brittany, but I was at least on the same floor. It was progress, and I knew by that point that my baby was a fighter. But even as the two of us began to recover, another part of my life was falling apart.

What I really wanted during those dark and anxious days was for someone to wrap me in their arms and tell me everything was going to be okay. Steve had never been that sort of person, so I didn't expect it from him. He stayed with me in my hospital room for the first four days, but when I moved up to maternity, he figured I was well enough that he could return to work. He'd always been a workaholic, so I wasn't surprised when, on the fifth day, he left to go on a business trip.

Throughout my entire life, it had been my dad who had played the role I needed now. He'd always been the person who would offer me words of wisdom and reassurance. He was the person who would tell me I was strong and could make it through the tough times, no matter what they were. I wanted that badly from him during those days in the hospital. And hasn't that happened to all of us? During those times when we need someone the most, the people who could help us are themselves too stretched to the limit or too scared or unaware to give us what they can't give themselves. As much as I longed to be comforted by my dad, it turned out that he needed comfort from me even more.

Weeks before I was rushed to the hospital to give birth to Brittany, I'd learned that my dad had had a relapse of his lymphoma. It was difficult news, but we'd also been through this already. After his initial diagnosis years before, Dad had gotten treatment and gone into remission, so I'd assumed the same thing would happen this time. That was what I thought up until the day before I gave birth to Brittany. That was when my dad's health had taken a turn for the worse, and he ended up in the hospital in Philadelphia at the same time that I was in the hospital in Florida.

The timing couldn't have been worse: one day prior to Brittany's emergency birth, I was admitted to the hospital after being diagnosed with preeclampsia. My doctor wanted to monitor me and the baby to make sure the preeclampsia didn't turn in to full eclampsia. My brothers were supposed to visit me in the hospital that day but they didn't show up, and I grew concerned. When I called them to find out where they were, they told me they hadn't come because they had to fly to Philadelphia to be with my dad.

My brothers didn't want to say too much at the time, because they knew I was dealing my own problems and they didn't want to add to my burden. They didn't tell me just how bad things had really gotten for my dad. Even so, I took the news hard.

It was because I was so upset about my dad that I'd begged my doctor to let me go home. I'd felt like I needed to be in familiar surroundings. I'd thought it would make me feel better, so I'd promised her I would stay in bed if she just let me go. And she had. It was just hours after she'd discharged me that I'd woken up in the middle of the night with horrible back and chest pains. That was how I'd ended up in the ER and then in the delivery room, experiencing the near loss of both my baby's life and my own that I've just described.

After Brittany's birth, the knowledge of what my family was going through at the same time made it even more difficult for me to recover. I kept picturing my dad lying in a hospital bed a thousand miles away at the same time that I was lying in mine. He wouldn't be able to show up at my bedside, wrap his arms around me, and tell me everything was going to be okay, like I wanted him to, so I knew I would have to go to him as soon as I was able. Mother Teresa once said, "I know God won't give me anything I can't handle." I'd always believed that before; but during those days, I wasn't so sure.

I talked to my doctors about wanting to see my father, and as soon as I was stable enough, they allowed me to leave Brittany in the care of the NICU and fly to Philadelphia for just a few hours to visit him. It was heartrending to leave my baby behind, especially since Steve was still away, but I knew I had to go. Until the cancer had crippled him, Dad had been a very successful banker, a hardworking provider for his family, and an amazing father. I worshipped the ground he walked on. Whenever I'd struggled with something, he had always encouraged me. Now I wanted to encourage him.

My sister and mom were already there when I arrived. While my siblings knew what had happened with me and Brittany, we kept the details from my parents. When I walked into Dad's hospital room, I could tell right away that he was heavily medicated. I put the biggest smile on my face that I could muster and did what I could to give him the kind of upbeat reassurance he'd always given me. Then I showed him a picture of Brittany that I'd taken before I'd left.

He looked at the picture of his newest granddaughter and said, "She is a beautiful Butler baby." Just hearing him say those words meant everything to me.

After I'd been there for a while, Dad's doctor came in. He greeted me and my family and, after he'd examined my dad, he asked us if we had any questions. I didn't say anything at the time, but after he left the room, something prompted me to follow him into the hall.

"Doctor?" I called after him. He stopped and turned around. I guess I was still looking for comfort of some kind, and I hoped this doctor would give it to me.

"Doctor," I continued when I caught up with him, "I'm getting back on a plane later today. My daughter is in the hospital, so I have to get back home. What reassurances can you give me that my dad is going to be okay?"

The doctor paused for a moment and just looked at me. Then he said quietly but firmly, "I'm sorry, but I can't give you any. At this point we're just trying to make him comfortable."

The words were like a punch in my gut. Until he said them, I hadn't realized just how sick Dad really was. He'd battled lymphoma before, and he'd gone into remission. I figured the same thing would happen this time as well. That is, until I heard those awful words that shattered all my hopes. Nothing would ever be the same again.

As the doctor walked away, I didn't know what to do. So I did the only thing I could think of: I kept going. I went back into my dad's room and said good-bye. I went back to the airport and got on a plane. I flew home to be with my baby in the hospital.

Ten days later, my dad died.

The Beginning of a Journey

That marked the beginning of the most tumultuous period of my life. Even after Brittany got better and was allowed to come home from the hospital, even after we buried my father and I returned home, even months later, I was still a wreck. All I wanted to do was stay in bed. Of course I was happy that Brittany and I had survived, but the recovery was difficult and the grief devastating. A dark fog hung over my head, and the feelings of sadness and loss were crushing. I had no energy or desire to get up and face the day. At the same time, I couldn't fall asleep or stop the negative thoughts from spinning through my head as I lay there trying. The voices in my head kept whispering things to me. I was anxious practically all the time, sure that something else was going to happen, that another traumatic event was just around the corner. "What's next?" was the refrain that kept playing over and over in my mind while I simultaneously put on my mask because I didn't want even my closest friends to know how much I was struggling. Only my family had any idea, and even some of them didn't know the extent of it. On the outside, I put on a brave face, but inside, I felt like I was living in a never-ending nightmare that left me both emotionally and physically incapacitated.

Deepak Chopra, a man who would later become a mentor to me and someone whose wisdom and personal friendship helped lead me to a better place, once said: "Even when you think you have your life all mapped out, things happen that shape your destiny in ways you might never have imagined."

Looking back now, I realize I had mapped out a picture-perfect life for myself, complete with high-powered husband, beautiful children, and a supportive extended family. I never expected the miscarriage, the near-death of both my daughter and myself, the loss of my beloved dad amidst it all, or any of the hardships to come. I not only had my dad to mourn during that time, but I was also mourning the lost vision of the life I'd always wanted. And who hasn't experienced that kind of mourning at least once (and probably a whole lot more than once) in their lives?

Over the next thirteen years, I faced many more heartaches—what I've told you so far is just the tip of the iceberg. But as you read on, you'll see that I did more than just survive it all. Ultimately, through many missteps and with lots of help along the way, I learned how to thrive. I stepped out of grief and back into the real world. I learned how to heal my body, my mind, and my spirit. As I began to heal myself, I also began to share my story. That helped me uncover my true life's purpose: to help you see that they don't have to live at the mercy of life's trials and tribulations. I believe we're all capable of living a life full of peace, love, and bliss, no matter what life throws at us along the way. My own experiences have given me some insight into how to do this and that's what I hope to share with you now.

A Guide for Finding Your Bliss

Not one of us is going to make it through this life unscathed. We will all suffer loss of one kind of another, be it the loss of a marriage, a loved one, a job, a dream we had for ourselves, or something else. We'll all deal with anxiety and stress over the difficulties of making it in this world. We'll all confront illness, depression, and heartache at one time or another. What's worse is that many of us will experience several of these things all at once. Do I sound like I have a pretty gloomy outlook on life? Well, I don't. I mention these things because I want you to know that they're nothing to be afraid of.

As I said before, when we're young, we're taught how to walk and talk, read and write, but there's no course in school that teaches us what to do when life feels insurmountable. When we've lost our way, how do we return to a place of peace, love, and bliss? When we lose ourselves, how do we get back to who we truly are?

I understand what it's like to be asking these kinds of questions, because I've asked them myself—many times—over the course of my life. I've gotten divorced (three times). I've lost loved ones under terrible circumstances. I've survived a cancer diagnosis and the loss of my dream of having more children. I've been through all these things and much, much more. In this book, I'll tell you what I've learned about getting through life's traumas, big and small, but this book is about more than that. My hope is that this book will be your guide, not just for getting through those hard times and healing yourself, but for going on to live a life full of bliss.

Ultimately, this is a book about finding peace and stability inside yourself, no matter what's happening on the outside. It's about recognizing that you have a right to be happy, no matter how badly you may think you've messed up. It's about feeling strong and empowered, about knowing who you are and what you want. And when you're living a life like that, when the hardships come—and they will come, because that's just life—you'll be ready for them. You can respond to them, learn from them, grow because of them, instead of having your world turned upside down by them, leaving you devastated and powerless.

It comes down to this: bad stuff happens. That's a reality that none of us can escape. What I hope to show you is that all that bad stuff doesn't have to stop you from living a life full of bliss.

CHAPTER TWO

What's Happening to Me?

"The greatest weapon against stress is our ability to choose one thought over another."

—William James, philosopher

Brittany remained in the hospital for two more weeks after I was discharged, during which time, I drove back and forth on a daily basis to be with her. When it finally came time to bring her home, I was both relieved and petrified. I was happy that she was well enough to be released, but I was also in a constant state of worry. She was still so very small and had lingering health issues, like kidney problems and acid reflux, a condition we discovered because whenever I would put her down to sleep, she would spit up her food. The doctors told me babies can choke on their own vomit and die when that happens, which only increased my level of fear and anxiety.

Then there were the unknowns. They still didn't know what the long-term effects might be of her traumatic early birth and being deprived of oxygen for several minutes. Would there be brain damage? Developmental problems? Something else? Something more? No one was entirely sure.

Steve was traveling on business when Brittany came home. I had my sister-in-law and, upon the doctor's recommendation, a nurse with me so I didn't have to be alone. And I needed the help. Besides all the typical activities that go with caring for a newborn, there were various medications to administer and frequent doctor visits to make. All in all, bringing my first child home from the hospital was not the joyous event I'd always imagined it would be. Instead, I was a nervous wreck. And that was even before I got the awful news, five days after Brittany's homecoming, that my father had died.

It was Steve who called to tell me. I assume that with everything that was going on, my family thought it best to tell him first. When I answered the phone, I thought he was just calling from the road to check in, but then he said to me in a quiet voice, "Pam, I think your dad died."

"What do you mean you 'think'?" I responded.

"Your dad died," he clarified, speaking more definitively this time.

And that was it. Ever since Brittany had come home from the hospital, I'd been feeling unsettled. I'd had this persistent, overwhelming sense that something bad was going to happen, that the other shoe was going to drop. When Steve gave me the news, I thought, *Well, here it is, the other shoe dropping.* There was no time to get too upset, no time to fall apart. I had to be there for my mom, my brothers, and my sister. I had to help plan a funeral. I couldn't leave Brittany behind, so I packed her up along with all the things she needed; and the very next day, we flew together, nurse in tow, to Philadelphia to be with my family.

The days that followed were a flurry of activity. I went with my mom to the funeral home to pick out a casket. Together, my family chose passages to be read and songs to be sung at the service. My two brothers, my sister, and I each wrote our own eulogy that we would read at the funeral. Through it all, I tried my best to support my mother while juggling Brittany's feedings, naps, medications, and everything else she needed. It was such a hard time for my mother. She had been en route to the hospital when my father finally passed, and she felt terribly guilty that she wasn't there for his final moments. Even before that, she'd been feeling badly that she couldn't be there with me for the birth of my first child. In fact, when we arrived in Philadelphia, my mom didn't even know the extent of what Brittany and I had been through. She was shouldering such a burden during those days that the whole family decided we didn't want to add to it by telling her more than she needed to know.

Somehow, I made it through those days, though to be honest, I'm not sure I could tell you exactly how. I remember doing a lot but feeling very little. It was like being on autopilot. Most of us have had the experience, at one time or another, of shutting down our emotions so we can simply make it through a difficult period. This is particularly common when we lose something or someone precious to us. It didn't really hit me until later that my dad was truly gone. That there would be no more hugs or inspirational chats. That for Brittany, there would be no memories of grandpa. That I would never again be able to turn to him during the tough times in my life and ask for his advice or comfort. That I would never again get to share all the wonderful things that happened in my life. Even today, it's hard to think about. Back then, I just couldn't think about it at all. So instead, I stopped feeling and sprang into action, did what I had to do, because really, what other choice do any of us have in situations like these? Survive and get through it. Sometimes that's all we can do.

Fight or Flight

When I heard the news that my dad had died, I immediately reverted to "go mode." There was no time to think, feel, or process what had happened, only to act, get done what needed to be done, and make it through the day. I'd done the exact same thing just a few weeks before when I'd learned my dad was in the hospital fighting for his life. Even though I had just been released from the hospital myself and was still recuperating from one of the most difficult experiences of my life—both physically and emotionally—I knew I had to get on a plane so I could be by his side, even if it was just for a little while. So that was what I did.

It was the same thing that had happened when Brittany was born: I woke up in the middle of the night with a sharp pain ripping through my body. I was scared to death and barely able to breathe, but I knew I had to get to the emergency room fast. So with Steve's help, I did. After that, I was focused only on survival—on mine, and even more importantly, on Brittany's.

Science has a name for how humans react in stressful moments like these. It's called "fight or flight mode" or "fight or flight response," a term coined by Walter Cannon, a physiologist and professor at Harvard Medical School, in the early twentieth century. Basically, it means that when our brains perceive that we're under some sort of threat, a signal is sent to our bodies to mobilize us for action. Our muscles tighten, our hearts race, our breath quickens, and we experience what is commonly known as an adrenaline rush. This is how we ready ourselves to either confront the threat (fight response) or turn and flee from it (flight response) in order to protect ourselves.

That was the state I was in during those trying days. Unfortunately, it was a state I got stuck in for quite some time afterward. Every time I was faced with another stressful situation—and they seemed to just keep coming—I pushed my feelings down deeper and deeper, while my body was always on guard to handle whatever came next. In the meantime, I couldn't sleep. My blood pressure was high and breathing was difficult. I was depressed, fearful, and filled with anxiety practically all the time.

If some or all of this sounds familiar, it's probably because it's quite common. Everyone experiences stress that sends them into fight or flight mode, at some time in their lives; and like me, many, many people experience it far more often than is good for them. This natural and necessary automatic process can do real harm to us if it's taken too far. And in the world we live in today, it's taken too far, far too often.

The Effect of Fight or Flight on Our Bodies and Minds

To get a better sense of how being stuck in fight or flight mode affects us, let's take a closer look at exactly what happens when it kicks into gear. It starts with our autonomic nervous system, which, in very basic terms, is that part of us that regulates our automatic or involuntary functions, like our heartbeat or digestion. Unless something is wrong with our bodies, we don't have to think about or make ourselves breathe, for example. It just happens all on its own, no matter what we're doing, no matter if we're awake or asleep.

Our sympathetic nervous system is one of the two main branches of our autonomic nervous system, and it's the part of the system responsible for that fight or flight response. That means that fight or flight is largely an unconscious reaction, something our bodies do automatically in response to stress. We don't tell ourselves to respond this way; we just do it.

When our fight or flight response is activated by stress, then our sympathetic nervous system sends signals throughout our bodies, and a whole host of things starts to happen. Our adrenal glands are stimulated, leading to more adrenaline and cortisol coursing through our systems. Our heart rate and breathing rate increase. Our platelets even get sticky, making our blood clot faster. And because it's more difficult to pump sticky platelets through our systems, our blood pressure rises as well.

Stress, and the physical reactions that come with it, serve an important purpose in certain situations. The cortisol that is released in our bloodstreams when we feel stressed, for example, is what gives us that extra energy we need to get to the hospital quickly or to get us through whatever trauma or difficult circumstance we're currently experiencing. The fact that our blood clots faster is a handy side effect if whatever happens to be causing us stress has also caused us bodily injury. We hear a lot about stress these days and what a terrible thing it is, but some stress really is a good thing. The problem starts when we get out of balance, when we become stressed too often, or when being stressed-out becomes our basic mode of operation. That can really drain the life right out of us.

When Fight or Flight Response Becomes a Problem

Once our sympathetic nervous system is activated, and our fight or flight response has kicked in, it can take some time before our bodies return to normal. And that's only if the brain thinks the threat is over. If that primitive or emotional part of our brain, which is connected to our sympathetic nervous system, continues to perceive a threat, then those reactions in our bodies can last much, much longer. And that's not a good thing.

As an example, let's look at the effect that raised cortisol levels can have on us. The extra energy that cortisol gives us is useful in an emergency, but cortisol levels are only meant to be elevated for a short period of time. When they stay elevated, it can negatively impact our sleep, our digestion, our immune function, and even our ability to produce other hormones. Add that to the overall impact of an elevated heart rate, blood pressure, breathing rate, and all the other physiological effects of fight or flight mode, and you can start to see how living this way can be very hard on us over time.

That's exactly what happened to me. Every time there was even a small window of opportunity to recuperate from one stressful event, I was hit with another. And then another.

Eventually, my body and brain just stayed ready for the next battle, the next crisis, the next tumultuous event in my life. After a time, my mind, body, and spirit were all wrecked, depleted, and exhausted. That was one of the biggest reasons why, after my father's funeral was finally over, after I'd handled it all, and Brittany and I were safely back home, I didn't begin to feel any better. Quite the opposite, I felt like I was spiraling out of control, and I didn't understand why. I didn't yet know all the things I just explained to you about fight or flight mode and the effects of stress, so I didn't understand what was happening to me as a result of all I'd been through. I certainly didn't know what to do about it, and I suffered even more because of that. A lot of people do, but it doesn't have to be that way.

We can all understand how fight or flight mode might come in handy if, say, we were being chased through the woods by a hungry mountain lion. To survive something like that, we would need our bodies to be ready, either to fight off that mountain lion or get away from it fast. Once upon a time, a situation like that may have been a very real threat for human beings. But today, most of us today don't face such dire circumstances very often.

That doesn't mean that our sympathetic nervous systems aren't kicking into gear on a regular basis and putting us in fight or flight mode. We still encounter stress, and our brains still perceive threats. But these days, the kinds of everyday "threats" that kick our sympathetic nervous systems into gear are more likely to be the non-life-threatening kind. They are much more likely to be everyday stresses, like the constant ping of our email when we're already feeling overwhelmed, the painfully slow commute when we just want to get home to our kids, or the big blowout we had with our spouse or partner over the household chores that ended in raised voices and hurt feelings.

My personal experience of living in chronic stress caused me to want to learn more about the effect it can have on people. After attending numerous lectures and reading up on the subject of stress, I've come to understand that the threats that stimulate our nervous systems can be either physical or—probably more common today—psychological, but unfortunately our automatic response system doesn't do a great job of distinguishing between good stress and bad stress, of determining which stresses are worth mobilizing the kind of physiological responses I described earlier (impending mountain lion attack or emergency trip to the hospital) and which are not (stuck in a traffic jam with nothing to do but get lose your mind!).

What that means is that, in many cases, our bodies are overacting to what's happening in our lives. That argument you just had with your teenage daughter may have been upsetting, but it's not going to kill you; so there's no real need for your body to ready itself to fight or run. Though it can be heart-wrenching, the loss of a loved one isn't something you need to battle or run from either, but your body still responds. These experiences alone won't kill us, but over time the stress we endure because of such events may very well end up killing us unless we learn to manage it.

Not only does stress have a damaging effect on our bodies over the long term, it also gets in the way of how we live on a daily basis. Over the long term, stress actually causes the amygdala—that part of the brain responsible for fight or flight mode—to grow larger, making it harder for us to recover from stress and making it so we stay in fight or flight mode even longer. At the same time, the hippocampus—the part of the brain responsible for decision making, memory, and even feelings of compassion—gets smaller. You can just imagine what effect this might have on a person's day-to-day functioning. According to Barbara Isanski's article, "Under Pressure: Stress and Decision Making," published by the Association for Psychological Science, research has shown that being under stress gets in the way of making quality decisions. Stress causes us to focus more on rewards and less on consequences, for example, which means if we're feeling stressed, we may do something impulsive to help us feel better in the moment (like reach for that cigarette or tub of ice cream), even though it isn't very good for us in the long run. Other negative impacts of stress include a reduction in our creativity, a reduction in our sense of objectivity, a reduction in our ability to think logically, and even a reduction in our ability to learn and communicate effectively. If you think about it, this means that being under stress really does reduce our quality of life, both physically and mentally, both short- and long-term.

Sadly, our bodies and minds don't come with an owner's manual, and how to manage stress isn't something we're typically taught in school. Too often we have to figure out how to do it all on our own. And if we don't figure it out, we suffer for it.

Top Causes of Stress

What stresses you out most in your life? In 2014, the American Institute of Stress reported the following seven things as the top causes of stress in people's lives.

1) Our jobs
2) Our finances
3) Our health
4) Our relationships
5) Poor eating habits (because what we put into our bodies affects our stress levels)
6) Our media habits, which can result in us too rarely giving our minds time to rest
7) Too little or poor quality sleep

How Common Is Stress?

Stress has become an epidemic in our society. It's become so common that many people believe they thrive on stress and drama. How often have you asked someone how they are, and they respond with someone like, "Oh, I'm so stressed out because I've got so much to do. I'm so busy that I don't have a moment to slow down!" But they don't say it like it's a bad thing. People often wear their stress like it's a badge of honor that shows just how important they really are.

The circumstances that have caused stress in your life might be very different from mine, but the effects of it and not knowing what to do about it are things that most people can relate to these days. Think about how you felt the last time you were stressed out for an extended period of time. The muscle aches. The headaches. The fatigue. The sleeplessness. The feelings of anxiety, fear, maybe even depression. These things are all quite common.

The American Institute of Stress reports that 77 percent of people regularly experience physical symptoms caused by stress, and 73 percent regularly experience psychological symptoms caused by it. That's a whole lot of people suffering from things like backaches, headaches, upset stomachs, muscle tension, changes in their sex drives, sleeplessness, irritability, moodiness, memory problems, and a whole host of other symptoms.

Major life changes like the death of someone close to you, the loss of a job, a divorce, or financial hardships can certainly cause stress, but more and more often, people are encountering stress in their daily lives: a long daily commute to and from the office; working long hours with few breaks; never unplugging from their phones, computers, or tablets; having too little time to connect with family and friends; never or rarely taking time for themselves or to relax. All in all, the evidence suggests that we are increasingly becoming overworked and overstressed, and it's taking its toll.

Amazingly, today *stress is the number one direct cause of illness in our society*. Stress does this by creating inflammation in body and brain, which can turn into disease. When you're stressed for a long period of time, it can seriously overwhelm your body, resulting in things like high blood pressure and high cholesterol. Stress also weakens your immune system, which makes it harder for the body to recover from illness or disease. Stress is a factor in just about all major illnesses, from cardiovascular disease, to autoimmune illnesses, to cancer.

But stress isn't just making our bodies less healthy. It's also affecting our minds and our spirits. When you're living on the edge, and your body is ramped up all the time, ready for battle, how do you think that makes you feel? Is that a state of being that's going to help you on your quest for more joy, more peace, more self-love? Is it going to make you feel more confident and secure, more energized and inspired? Is it going to make you feel more loving and compassionate toward other people? The answer to all of these questions is almost surely no.

The real questions we need to ask ourselves are: Do we want to continue living this way? Do we want to be go-go-going all the time? Does that make us feel good about ourselves and our lives? If we're honest with ourselves, the answer has to ultimately be no.

It's clear that while some stress is good, living a stressed-out life isn't good for any of us. Of course, understanding that and doing something about it are two very different things. But we can start by noticing or being mindful of the toll that stress is taking on us—mentally, physically, emotionally, and spiritually. The next thing we can do is begin to understand that we don't have to live this way. We don't have to live with so much drama. Stress, trauma, hardships, death, illness, sadness—these are all facts of life, but how we choose to prepare ourselves for, react to, and interact with these major forces makes all the difference. This whole book is about that very idea, but before you learn anything else, it's important to understand that there is another way. You don't have to live a stressed-out life anymore.

Mindfulness means becoming more aware of the present moment, of noticing what's happening right now, inside of you and in the world around you.

Pause and Take Notice

How often have you plowed through a difficult time at work, only the end up with a splitting headache at the end of the day? Or a trying morning with the kids that leaves you feeling utterly spent and empty? Or you force yourself to ignore your precarious finances, failing relationship, or other situation that you feel ill-equipped to deal with, only to end up feeling weighted down, anxious or fatigued (or all of the above and more)? We often don't even notice when we're taking on too much, when we're getting worked up, when stress starts to set in. We don't notice until it's already overwhelmed us.

Before we can decide to make any sort of change in our lives, first we have to *pause and take notice*. We can't change what we cannot see. And one of the big problems with getting stuck in fight or flight mode is that it primes us for action, not reflection. We're often too busy just getting through the day to notice what *just* getting through it is doing to us.

So that's where we're going to start; by practicing what's called *mindfulness*. I'm sure you've heard this word before, used in all sort of different contexts, but for our purposes here, I define it as taking the time to become aware of the present moment, to notice what's happening both inside of you and in the world around you. That's particularly important at this stage of our journey because no one can make a change if they don't see the need. When we're out of balance, our bodies and minds give us all sorts of signs—those headaches, muscle aches, feelings of fatigue, anxiety, or depression. The problem is, either we don't notice the signs, or we ignore them. Too often, we do this until it's too late, and they've really taken a toll on us.

As I mentioned in the introduction, this book is full of tools to help you on your journey, things you can do to hijack your mind and body, disrupt negative patterns, and practice bringing transformation into your life. The very first tool I want to give you is STOP, which comes from Daniel Siegel, MD, a clinical professor of psychiatry at the UCLA School of Medicine. Simply put, the STOP tool is about stopping for a moment. Stop moving, stop doing, stop thinking, stop trying, stop go-go-going. Instead, take some time to just breathe. After that, sit and observe yourself for a bit. Observe your physical body. Observe your mental and emotional state. Ask yourself: How am I doing right now?

If you're in the midst of dealing with a difficult situation, how are you handling it? If that's too much to think about, and you start feeling overwhelmed, then just play the "name that sensation" game. Notice what you're feeling—mentally, physically, emotionally—and try to put a name to it. Are you feeling worried? Achy? Tired? Angry? There are no wrong answers, and this doesn't have to take a lot of time. Just spend a few moments checking in with yourself. This will set you up to begin practicing the mindful breathing techniques that follow, which will help you begin to relieve some of that stress that's getting in the way of your living the fullest life possible.

S.T.O.P.

Use this tool anytime you're starting to feel overwhelmed or just feel the need to check in with yourself and be mindful of what's happening to and around you. Each letter stands for a simple step, which Siegel broke down as follows:

S is for "stop." Whatever is happening, whatever you're doing, just stop for a moment.

T is for "take three deep breaths." Breathe in really big through your nose. Then open your mouth and exhale. Do this three times in a row.

O is for "observe." Observe what's going on. Notice your breath. Notice what's going on inside of you. Notice the world around you. Maybe even notice the person you're with, if you happen to be with someone. Don't judge or dwell on these things. Just observe them.

P is for "proceed with loving kindness and compassion." Whatever you choose to do next, whether it's the breathing techniques that follows or just continuing to go about your day, have the intention that you will do so in a spirit of love and compassion.

Your Bliss Toolbox: Stop, Drop, and Breathe

We breathe every day, all the time, but how often do we pay attention to our breath? How often do we breathe mindfully or with intention? For most people, the answer is not very often or maybe even never.

Life can be stressful, but thankfully, our bodies come with a built-in stress reliever: our breath. And yet, so many of us have been breathing incorrectly all our lives. Holding our breaths through stress and difficulty when what we really need is more air. Or taking quick, choppy breaths when we're nervous or unset when what we really need is to slow our breath down to bring our nervous system back into balance. Research shows that paying attention to our breath has a wide range of extraordinary benefits. In fact, real transformation in our lives can happen one breath at a time.

First, taking long, slow, conscious breaths helps slow down both your mind and your body. If you're stuck in fight or flight mode, slowing down your breath is a great way to start bringing yourself out of it and reducing the amount of stress you're feeling.

Next, breathing in a deep, relaxed way has been shown to have all sorts of health benefits. It can have a positive impact your heart, your immune system, your digestion, your respiratory system, even your brain.

Finally, when you're engaged in the kind of focused, intentional breathing techniques that follow, you have to concentrate on what you're doing. That forces you to be present, rather than thinking about the past or future. A lot of depression lies in thoughts from the past—the "shoulda, coulda, woulda" thoughts. A lot of anxiety lies in thoughts of the future, the unknown or fear of what might happen. Focusing on your breath makes it so you can't live in any moment other than the present one. And if you're completely focused on the present, it's going to be pretty hard to feel anxious or depressed.

The following breathing techniques are a great place to start when you're having a hard time and know you need to find a way out of it. They are all quick and easy so that anyone can do them, no matter what's happening in their lives, no matter how much stress and pressure they're under, no matter how short they are on time. They are a great way to hijack or disrupt destructive patterns in your mind or body and reset yourself. All for doing something you already do every day, all day, but this time with just a bit more focus and intention.

Get Ready to Breathe

To practice any of the following techniques, simply begin by getting comfortable. Sit up nice and tall in a comfortable chair or on the floor. You can choose to have your eyes open or closed. Just do what feels most natural to you.

Next, relax your body as much as possible. Do an internal body scan from head to toe, letting go of any tension in your neck, shoulders, back, or wherever you happen to carry it. Do that as much as you can before you start your breathing techniques.

Finally, remember to go easy on yourself. There is no right or wrong way to practice these techniques. The main idea is to try them, then notice what's happening to you as a result. And then just keep practicing. As with anything else, breathing in a new way takes practice. I like to compare it to a child learning to play a musical instrument. In the beginning, it may be hard for the child, and she may feel like she's not very good at it. She may even be right. But the more she practices, the better she gets. She may start off with "Chopsticks," and then one day find herself playing Chopin—but it will only happen with practice.

If you've been breathing quick, shallow breaths all your life, it might take some time before these techniques start to feel right to you. But just like with playing an instrument, or anything else you're learning to do, the more you practice, the easier it will be. And the easier it becomes, the more satisfaction you will gain from it.

Technique #1: Sweet Sixteen Breath

This is a supereasy starter that you can use in everyday life whenever you're feeling stressed or anxious. It's also a favorite of my now teenage daughter, Brittany, who found it especially useful for managing stress when she was in her senior year of high school and applying to colleges. She even wrote about it in one of her college application essays, explaining, "This exercise brings awareness to your breath, which takes you into the present moment. When we are mindful of our breathing and counting our breath, we can't be worried or stressed about anything else at the same time. Personally, I have found when I take the time to stop and become more mindful with what I'm doing, my stress seems to dissolve."

When I read that, I was so proud that my daughter already understood the importance of keeping her stress and anxiety in check. It was also a reminder that a person can experience stressful feelings at any age, so it's never too early to start learning ways to manage them. This technique can help anyone learn how to slow down their breath and quiet their mind. It's a sixteen-second breath, with four counts for each stroke, as follows:

1) With your mouth closed, inhale slowly through your nose for a count of 4-3-2-1.
2) Hold the breath for a count of 4-3-2-1.

3) With your mouth closed, exhale slowly through your nose for a count of 4-3-2-1.
4) Hold the breath for a count of 4-3-2-1.

Repeat this sixteen-second breath as many times as you want until you feel your mind and body start to settle down. When you've finished, you might want to ask yourself: Was I able to think about anything in the past or anything coming up in the future? The answer will almost surely be no.

Technique #2: 4-7-8 Breath

This is a technique I learned from Dr. Andrew Weil, a leader in the field of integrative medicine. I find it's a great one to try when I'm having trouble sleeping. It really helps me relax and calm down my systems so I can get some rest. It involves inhaling through the nose and then exhaling though the mouth in the following way:

1) Inhale through your nose for a count of 4-3-2-1.
2) Hold the breath for a count of 7-6-5-4-3-2-1.
3) Purse your lips and blow out slowly through your mouth for a count of 8-7-6-5-4-3-2-1.

Repeat the 4-7-8 breath as many times as you need until your start feeling relaxed. Make sure not to get too caught up in thinking that you can't do it or it's too difficult. For example, at first, some people have a hard time holding their breath for a count seven. That's okay. If you're having trouble, you can simply lessen the number, holding for a count of four or five, until you build up lung capacity. It may take some practice, but the most important thing is that you make the effort and notice what happens as a result.

Technique #3: Left Nostril Breathing

This technique, too, is a good one to try if you're having trouble sleeping, but it's really something you can do anytime, anywhere: If you're stuck in traffic. If you're feeling stressed out at work or at home. You can even do it in public and people will hardly notice.

The idea is to tap into your parasympathetic nervous system. I spoke earlier about our sympathetic nervous systems, which is responsible for that fight or flight response. The opposite of that is our parasympathetic nervous system, which is responsible for more calming and soothing feelings. Your right nostril is connected to your sympathetic nervous system, while your left nostril is connected to the parasympathetic nervous system. You can tap into that calming parasympathetic nervous system by doing the following:

1) Place a finger on your nose to close off your right nostril.
2) Breathe in and out through your left nostril, taking long, slow, deep breaths.

I like to do this at night just before bed, in conjunction with a leg-up-the-wall yoga pose. I lie on the floor with my legs in the air, leaning up against the wall, and close off my right nostril. (See chapter 7 for more on this yoga pose.) I breathe this way for a while, until I'm feeling good and relaxed and ready for sleep.

Technique #4: Anxiety-Buster Breath

I learned this technique at a retreat given by life coach, author, and speaker Gabrielle Bernstein. She calls it her anxiety-buster exercise, and I've found that it works great for my anxiety. You can help manage your own anxiety by doing the following:

1) Stop whatever you're doing and find a place where you can sit for a few moments without being disturbed.
2) Inhale through your nose for eight short, staccato breaths.
3) Blow out the breath in one forceful count through your mouth.

You will be able to hear your breaths as they go in and out—first the short, clipped inhales ones after the other, and then the big whoosh of air going out. Repeat this breathing technique until your anxiety starts to wane.

If you practice these four breathing techniques every day and then take the time to stop and observe yourself, you will start to notice the benefits to your body and mind. You can begin to shift your whole nervous system with just your breath. That can mean less time spent in fight or flight mode, a reduction in your overall level of stress, and fewer of the negative physiological effects that I talked about in this chapter. It can also mean a calmer, more relaxed state of being, which will help you make the kind of positive choices I will talk about in the next chapter—ones that can take you from a life of stress and anxiety to one filled with peace, love, and bliss, no matter what tough circumstances may come your way!

CHAPTER THREE

Choosing Change

"With everything that has happened to you, you can either feel sorry for yourself or treat what has happened as a gift. Everything is either an opportunity to grow or an obstacle to keep you from growing. You get to choose.*"*

—**Dr. Wayne Dyer**

You might think that once I returned home after my dad's funeral, I would have finally begun to recover—physically, mentally, and emotionally—from the whirlwind of things I'd been through since Brittany was born. That was what I was hoping for too. I thought that I would finally have time to settle back into the life I'd been living before. But the exact opposite happened. When I got home, I no longer had an emergency situation on my hands to keep my mind and body go-go-going all day long. When I finally slowed down and had some time to myself, well ... that was when the worst set in.

You have no doubt encountered your own days when it was hard to get out of bed in the mornings. Or, when you went to bed at night, you found it difficult to fall asleep because you were overcome with anxiety about the state of your life. Like me, you may have experienced both these feelings interchangeably, one after the other like they were dueling for supremacy. When I wasn't anxious, I was depressed, thinking about all the things I was missing out on now that my dad was gone. When I wasn't depressed, I was anxious, worried about what could possibly come next.

One day, it dawned on me that I would never be able to tell my dad—the person who had always been my hero, my champion, my consolation—everything that I'd been through during the past months. I would never be able to tell him about how Brittany had nearly died, about how I had nearly died myself, about all the fear and sadness that had followed. He was the person who had always assured me that everything was going to be okay, but now he would never say those words to me again. And this time around, I really wasn't sure that everything was going to be okay. I wasn't sure of that at all.

It was one of those brought-to-your-knees kind of moments. I was anxious about Brittany, who still had a lot of recovery to go through. I was depressed about my dad, whom I hadn't had a chance to say good-bye to or to mourn properly. I had my own physical trauma from Brittany's birth to recover from, not to mention the fact that as a new mother, my hormones were pretty out of whack. And basically, I was dealing with it all on my own. My family, especially my mother, had their own grief to deal with. My husband was a hardworking business executive who spent long hours at the office and on the road.

It was like I was alone in the woods, lost without a map, and I just didn't know how to cope.

Not that I let anyone see that I was feeling that way. So many of us have gotten so good at hiding our feelings away and pretending to the world outside that nothing is wrong. Whenever I did go out, whenever I did talk to someone, I forced a smile on my face and put on the mask of "everything's okay!" I had always aimed to be the perfect daughter, then the perfect wife, and now the perfect mother. But suddenly, I found myself failing to live up to that image I had of myself, and I didn't want anyone else to see.

One night when I was putting Brittany down to sleep, I remember feeling so incredibly overwhelmed by it all that I just couldn't pretend anymore that everything was all right. We were still managing her acid reflux with medication, but when I looked at her lying there in her crib, I couldn't stop thinking that she might throw up, choke, and die in the middle of the night. I couldn't get to sleep because that thought kept running through my head. I kept checking on her, over and over again, to make sure she was okay. In the meantime, my heart was fluttering, and my breathing grew increasingly short and choppy until it felt like I wasn't getting enough oxygen. I didn't know it at the time, but I was in the midst of a full-blown panic attack.

Of course, Brittany made it through the night just fine, but I didn't. The next morning I was a mess, and it wasn't the first time I had felt that way. Yet, I didn't share these kinds of feelings with anyone except my family. Even my closest friends, some of whom had babies of their own, didn't know. I turned to my girlfriends for distractions from my pain rather than getting "down and dirty" with them about how I was really feeling. I wanted to be just like everyone else, so I did what I knew how to do best—I kept moving, kept busy, kept pretending that the pain didn't exist, kept smiling as if everything were fine. But things weren't fine. I wasn't fine. I was so lonely and lost, and with my husband often away, I felt like I didn't have anyone to share my insecurities with.

I think many of us adopt this kind of social mask during difficult times. It's like a kind of suit of armor we put on to protect ourselves. But wearing something like that all the time is a lot of work, and we won't ever be able to get at our real essence when we're hiding ourselves in this way. Soon after that night when I had a panic attack, I decided I just couldn't take it any longer. I wasn't functioning. I was fed up with feeling panicky all the time. I needed to get some sleep. Most of all, I knew I couldn't take care of my daughter like that.

About four months after Brittany was born, I finally made a choice. Something had to change, so I went to see a therapist. When I showed up for my first appointment, the mask was gone. I was a wreck, and I let him see it. By that point, I'm not sure I could have hidden it anymore even if I'd wanted to.

To my surprise, my therapist diagnosed me with post-traumatic stress disorder (PTSD). I had many of the common symptoms that PTSD sufferers endure, including recurring, unwanted flashbacks of what I'd been through during Brittany's delivery and then with my dad. I had trouble sleeping, and when I did sleep, I often had nightmares. I avoided places, activities, and people that I'd enjoyed before, and my thinking had become extremely negative, often fearful that more bad things were coming just around the corner. When I wasn't feeling depressed, anxious, or afraid, I just felt numb. There was no joy in my life.

I felt so numb, in fact, that when he gently said to me, "Pam, I believe that you are suffering from post-traumatic stress disorder," I barely reacted. I didn't feel shock or surprise. I didn't feel relief that I finally had a name for what I was going through. I didn't feel much of anything. He wanted to start me on medication to treat it, so I accepted that, too, without question, or even a reaction. I simply took the prescription and went on my way.

It was a small, quiet moment, but it was still a turning point for me. Ultimately, I would find a different, more sustainable path to healing, but for the time being, the medication I took and the talk therapy appointments I went to over the coming weeks and months cracked open a window for me. The pills dulled some of the pain, and I was finally able to get some sleep. The fog gradually began to lift after that. And that was a starting place, a small first step on what would become a new life's path for me.

Taking a First Step

I wish I could tell you that I had some kind of big epiphany, one where I stood up defiantly, fist in the air, and said, "I will live this way no more!" Perhaps that's how change will come for you, but it wasn't how it happened for me. There wasn't some big dramatic moment. It was more like a series of small choices. I chose to get out of bed. I chose to seek some help from a therapist. I chose to show up at the therapist's without the mask I usually wore and be completely honest with him.

It was this series of small choices made—and small choices I would continue to make—that put me on a new path.

I also wish I could tell you that I chose to make these changes for myself because I understood that I wanted a better life than the one I was living. But I didn't. Later on, I would make that kind of choice for myself, but at the time, I did it for my daughter. Brittany was both my compass and my life jacket. She was only a few months old at the time, and I was home alone with her, trying to take care of her through it all. I was trying to respond to her cries, make sure she was fed, keep up with her medications and doctor visits, all while I was finding it hard to even get out of bed each morning. I felt like I was not functioning well as a mother, and I just couldn't accept that. Brittany needed me, so I needed to be able to be there for her.

I tell you this because even though the first baby steps on my path to something more may have been far from ideal, they still took me somewhere better. It would have been nice had I felt fully empowered and deserving when I made the choice to live differently. It would have been nice had I felt ready to blaze my own path back to my true self. But in the beginning, I was numb and powerless, and I let my therapist guide me. Sometimes, when life brings you to your knees, you simply need to concentrate on finding a way to stand up before you can run.

We're not perfect creatures after all, so any path we walk, any choices we make are not going to be perfect either. And that's okay. The main thing to focus on is that you always have a choice. You can always choose to do things differently, no matter what's going on in your life. Depending on your circumstances and what state you're in, you may choose to make a change in a big way or a small one, but real change can start either way. Wayne Dyer, the late motivational speaker and author who was a big source of inspiration for me as well as many, many others, once said, "With everything that has happened to you, you can either feel sorry for yourself or treat what has happened as a gift. Everything is either an opportunity to grow or an obstacle to keep you from growing. You get to *choose*." I have come to truly believe that.

I wasn't sure exactly where I wanted to end up when I started seeing a therapist. I wasn't sure exactly how I was going to get there either. But I had hit a fork in the road, and I knew one thing for certain: I couldn't continue in my life the way I was living it. I wanted to be better for my daughter, so I chose change. I chose to do something differently one day by admitting I needed help and going out and seeking it.

It may not sound like a lot, but it was a first step. And every journey begins with just one step. Too often, we wait to make changes in our lives until we can see exactly how those changes, all laid out in front of us, are going to play out. But if you do that, then change can take too long. And, in fact, it may never come.

If you are feeling like life has you by the scruff of the neck, I want to encourage you not to look too far down the road. When life overwhelms you, it's often best to look only at the next step you need to take. If you're suffering, choose to say, "I no longer want to suffer." If you're living a stressed-filled, on-the-go lifestyle, choose to say, "I want to slow down." If you're feeling lost and alone, choose to say, "I will ask for and accept help." If you're in a situation that you don't want to be in any longer, choose to say, "I don't want to do this anymore."

The point is that you don't always have to know exactly what you're doing before you do something or where you're going before you go somewhere different. If you can't see the forest for the trees (first, join the club!), then simply choose, not a path, not a destination, but to change. Choose to see trauma and hardship as an opportunity to grow instead of an obstacle keeping you in your current circumstances. During those brought-me-to-my-knees moments in my life, I found that idea empowering. You can simply choose change. Whatever that ends up meaning. And that alone can be enough to get you started.

Finding Your Inspiration

You probably recognize the feeling that things just can't continue the way they have been for much longer, even if you don't know how to change them. That was how I felt when I finally went to see a therapist. It was like I had been flailing about in the water for too long and it was time to either sink or swim. I wanted to be able to care for my daughter, and I chose to keep my head above water, not for me, but for her. I held on to Brittany as my inspiration and motivation through all the barriers that someone faces when trying to make a real change in their lives.

If you're looking to make a similar kind of change in your life, it's important to understand not just that you want to make that change, but *why* you want to make it. Think about what your own inspiration could be, what might keep you going when times get tough. It doesn't have to be the perfect reason (whatever that is), it just has to be something that drives you. Maybe you want to make a change for yourself. Maybe you want to do it for your partner or your family. Maybe health issues or other circumstances are forcing the need for a change in your life. Whatever the reason, it's important to know what's motivating you right now. Of course, motivations can change, as they did for me, but understanding and being mindful of what's motivating you will give you a touchstone, something to hold on to when you confront the inevitable barriers to change that will come.

If you're having trouble thinking of a specific person or reason for choosing change, then you might want to ask yourself a question that I often pose to students and clients. Really think about your current approach to life and then ask yourself: How's that working out for me? You might also want to ask: How is that working for the people around me, the people I love and care about? If the answer to either or both of those questions is "not well," then what's keeping you from trying something different?

When we're stuck in fight or flight mode, when we're stressed out and always on the go, we often don't take time to stop and ask ourselves questions like those. That's why the breathing techniques I described in the last chapter can be so helpful. They force us to slow down, giving us time and space to consider what's going on in our lives and ask ourselves important questions. Change takes time, space, and consideration, so you have to start by creating these kinds of moments for yourself. They are moments of opportunity to see or do things differently.

The biggest barrier to change is often basic inertia. It's a powerful force. As human beings, we get into habits that we feel comfortable with, even if they're bad habits. Techniques like breathing, and the other tools you will discover in the coming chapters, help us to be mindful and be in the present. They help us to slow down so we can really look at our lives. The definition of insanity is doing the same thing over and over again and expecting a different result. You've probably heard that before, and yet we all behave this way. But the truth is, if we really don't like things the way they are, then we have to start thinking about doing things differently. We can't just continue on our current course and expect things to get better.

Another powerful force that keeps us from making a change is fear: What if I'm not capable of change? What if what's around the corner is actually worse than where I am now? What if I don't deserve more than what I have right now? Fear often comes to us as these kinds of gnawing questions. But fear isn't something we need to avoid. It's something we need to learn to live with and listen to. If you find yourself feeling fearful about making a change, just sit with that feeling for a moment. (You'll find some tools to help you do this at the end of this chapter.) And then remember the old saying about FEAR, which is that it stands for "false evidence appearing real." Maybe fear is telling you that you can't do this, or that things will be worse if you do, but remember that you have no evidence of that. How will you know until you try?

It's important for us all to be aware of what's happening to us when we feel fear. In the last chapter, I described how our sympathetic nervous system all too often kicks into gear when we don't really need it to. If we're under attack by terrorists, sure, we should feel fearful. But in today's world, the vast majority of the time what we fear is something that's not going to kill us. We fear that no one will love us. We fear that we're not good enough. We fear that we're not strong enough. We fear things that aren't really there and aren't really true. We fear outcomes that we can't possibly know will happen until we try. That's why it's so important to know how to breathe through the moments when we're feeling depressed, anxious, or fearful. If we can slow ourselves down long enough to notice what's happening to us and how we're feeling, then we can choose how we want to react. That's how we create space for change.

My Inspiration to You: To Live in Bliss

If you're having trouble finding your own inspiration to make a change, I'd like to suggest one that I wish I'd had back when I was living in my perfect storm of back-to-back traumas. Think about what your life is like now. Maybe you've experienced trauma recently, like I had. Maybe you're overly stressed and are sent in fight or flight mode at the drop of a hat. Maybe you feel like you're at the mercy of your schedule, your responsibilities, your high-octane lifestyle. Maybe you just can't stop feeling anxious and overwhelmed. Or sad and unfulfilled. Instead of living life like that, imagine what it would be like to live a life filled with *bliss*.

What is bliss exactly? Joseph Campbell once described it this way: "The way to find out about happiness is to keep your mind on those moments when you feel most happy, when you are really happy—not excited, not just thrilled, but deeply happy. This requires a little bit of self-analysis. How would you describe bliss? What is it that makes you happy? Stay with it, no matter what people tell you. This is what is called following your bliss."

I personally define *bliss* as that special place inside all of us, the place where we can find real peace, love, and joy. Bliss is not so much a thing as it is a state of being. What's more, it's a state of being that no one can take away from us, unless we let them. It's a state of being that no outside forces or events can shake, unless we let them. That's because bliss comes not from some external source of power or validation, but from inside ourselves. It comes from connecting to that higher sense of who we are and loving that true part of us.

When I was diagnosed with PTSD, I was basically limping through life. Everyday activities that I'd done a thousand times in my life were suddenly excruciatingly difficult, like getting out of bed or taking the dog for a walk. I remember my brother looking at me one day and saying that I really needed some fresh air, so he suggested we take the dogs for a walk. I didn't want to admit to him how hard that sounded to me at the time—imagine, a leisurely walk down the street feeling like a chore!—so I took half a Xanax just to get myself out the door. Back then, living the kind of life I have just described was something I couldn't even imagine. But I wish I could have. Because it was exactly what I needed in my life.

The thing about living in bliss is that you draw your power, inspiration, and fulfillment from inside of yourself, so even when the worst happens, you can handle it. You're more resilient because you have that place, that well of strength inside of you to return to whenever you need it. And then, when the good times come, you can enjoy them even more because you're living from a place of bliss.

Before the voice in your head tells you that you're never going to be able to have something like that, let me assure you that bliss is a state of being that we're all capable of reaching. It doesn't matter how old we are, what belief system we subscribe to, what we've done in the past, or how difficult our circumstances may be. It takes some effort to get there, but we all have the capacity, and it's worth the effort. None of us can control what happens in our lives. Loved ones die, we get sick, relationships fail, companies lay off employees, and on and on and on. Trauma and hardship are an unavoidable part of the human condition. We can't control many things in life, but what we do have some control over is what happens inside us. Since I found my way to bliss, I still suffer, but I suffer less now because I know how to recover more quickly. When bad things happen in my life, I know they are just things that are happening to me; they no longer define me or my life. And when things are good, they're made even better by the sense of peace, love, joy, and gratitude that I carry with me every day.

Wouldn't you rather live a life like that? I'm sure you would, because who wouldn't? And you can. If I could climb out of that place of despair I was living in and find my way here, then you can too. How to do that is what the rest of this book is about; but for now, just know that bliss is well within your reach. So take a moment to consider what it might be like to live a life filled with it.

What Is Bliss?

Dictionaries define *bliss* as a state of extreme happiness, ecstasy, or spiritual joy. I would add to that definition that bliss is a utopian state of being that can only be found within yourself. When you connect to who you truly are and learn to love and embrace that person fully, then you will find that state of peace, love, and joy.

Recording Your Journey

A great way to signal to yourself that you're ready to make a change and start a new journey in your life—whatever it may be—is by keeping a journal. Early on in my own journey to find myself, I started keeping one at the suggestion of one of my teachers. At the time, my mind was so congested with so many thoughts swirling anxiously about that I really needed a place to put them. I found that I could use my journal as a tool for simply unloading them and clearing space. I would sit down, set a timer for five minutes, and perform what I called a "mind dump," writing whatever came to mind, whether it was an expression of what I was feeling, stories of what I'd been through that day, new ideas I'd read about or thought up myself, or something else. It didn't matter so much what I wrote, but the act of writing helped me slow down and process my thoughts, and then open up space in my mind.

Writing about one's thoughts and experiences in a journal, log, or diary is practically as old as writing itself. It's a practice that's been common among presidents of the United States, famous authors, ship captains, and teenage girls, among many other groups. As it turns out, there are good reasons why so many people have found it a worthy way to pass the time. Researchers in recent years have found that journal keeping can actually benefit our health and well-being. Various studies have shown that it helps us relieve stress, set and achieve goals, enhance memory, improve relationships and communication with others, and more. There is even evidence of some direct health benefits. Through research done at the University of Austin, psychologist James Pennebaker found that writing regularly boosted immune function in study participants ("Writing to Heal," *Monitor on Psychology*).

Just like I coached in the last chapter when I introduced you to some breathing techniques, when it comes to starting a journal, it's important not to judge yourself. We're not aiming for Shakespeare here. A journal is simply a tool you can use to record what's happening to and around you, to release your thoughts and feelings, to try out new ideas, and even to make promises to yourself. This is a safe space for you and you alone, so keep that in mind as you begin your journal-keeping practice. And remember to keep your journal in a sacred place!

Your Bliss Toolbox: Mindful Journaling

You can buy a nicely bound journal if you wish, but an empty notebook will do just as well. It's great if you have a person in your life with whom you can confide, but that doesn't mean you can't benefit from journaling as well. Remember that the blank page doesn't judge, and you don't have to worry about its feelings. You can simply take the weight off your shoulders and dump it, along with all your other thoughts, onto the piece of paper, without thinking too much about it. The blank page gives you permission to be as raw and honest as you want to be.

I would encourage you to try to write something every day, even if it's just a line or two about what's happened. Before you sit down to start writing, it can be a good idea to do some of the breathing techniques from the last chapter to slow yourself down and put yourself in a writing frame of mind. Then set a timer for five minutes or more and just let the thoughts fly. If you're having trouble figuring out what to write, the following journal prompts can get you started. Even if you don't have any trouble figuring out what to say, these journal prompts are a good way to start being mindful of what kind of changes you want to make in your life and what barriers might be standing in your way. So give them a try.

Journal Prompt #1: **Name Your Fears**

I mentioned earlier in this chapter how fear often stands in the way of us making a change in our lives. Too often, fear remains some amorphous but powerful force in our heads that we feel but never take time to understand. This writing exercise aims to give those feelings a name.

Begin by simply creating a list in your journal of what you're afraid of. When you think about making a change in your life, what fears start to bubble to the surface?

It's important not to judge your thoughts, or yourself, as you write. Just name the fears that come to mind and write them down. If a thought or two comes to you about each fear, like where the fear comes from or the last time you felt it, jot that down as well. When you're finished, take a moment to reflect on whether naming your fears and writing them down took some of the power away from them.

Journal Prompt #2:
Leave Your Stress on the Page

As we learned in chapter 2, it's important to be mindful of the stressors that could be sending you into fight or flight mode, a state of mind that makes change very difficult. In your journal, take some time to write about what is stressing you out. Write down everything you can think that has made you feel this way recently.

Next, ask yourself: What did I feel like when I was experiencing that particular stressor? Describe what you felt physically, mentally, and emotionally during each instance. This will help you become more mindful of what's happening to you the next time your sympathetic nervous system kicks into gear, and perhaps make a choice to react differently to that stressor in the future.

Journal Prompt #3:
Paint a Picture of Your Future

There's an exercise I like to play with my students or people in my workshops who are on the brink of making a change. It's called the future-self exercise, and it's pretty simple. It entails sitting quietly for a moment, then imagining your future self. Once you've done that, imagine that your future self gives you a gift. What would it be?

In your journal, record what that gift might be. Describe it in as much detail as you can and why your future self might be giving it to you. Then you can take your writing a step further and imagine what your future self is like and what life is like for your future self. Ask yourself the following questions:

What does your future self look like and sound like?

If, in the future, your future self has the life you truly want, what does it look like? Where do you live? What do you do? Who surrounds you? What do you have then that you don't have now?

How does your future self feel about your life? How does your future self feel about him or herself? How does your future self feel about the past you, the person you are now?

CHAPTER FOUR

Finding Your Own Path

"Faith is a place of mystery, where we find the courage to believe in what we cannot see and the strength to let go of our fear of uncertainty."

—Brené Brown

One day, not long after my PTSD diagnosis, I started talking to a friend about what I was going through. I told him about Brittany's birth and my father's death. I told him what had happened to me afterward and a little bit about what I'd been doing to try to recover. I also told him that, while I was feeling better, I wasn't getting the kind of results I'd been hoping for with therapy and the various medications I'd been prescribed.

"I just feel like there has to be another way to treat myself," I said to him. I had no idea what that way might be, but I knew I wanted something more. As it turned out, I had stumbled on the right person to talk to about all this.

The person I was talking to happened to be a personal friend of Deepak Chopra, the physician whose focus on integrative medicine and the mind-body connection had brought him to the world's attention. At that point in my life, I knew very little about that sort of thing. I'd heard Chopra's name before in passing, but that was about it. But then my friend started talking to me about how Chopra, who had been trained as a medical doctor, believed that the medical profession was doing people a disservice by treating the body as if it were somehow separate from the mind. Of course, my friend only scratched the surface of Chopra's work in the course of our casual conversation, but what he was describing immediately appealed to me. I was feeling both open-minded enough and desperate enough to try something completely new. And in that moment, it sounded to me like that was exactly what Chopra was offering: a new path to healing.

My friend recommended a visit to the Chopra Center for Wellbeing in Carlsbad, California, not far from San Diego, and I booked a trip the first chance I got. Brittany was about six months old when we traveled together across the country to Southern California to visit what would turn out to be a life-changing place.

The moment I arrived in Carlsbad, I fell in love with the place. The sunshine. The vast blue of the ocean. The relaxed vibe and people. And that was even before I arrived at the Chopra Center. When I walked into the Center for the first time, I felt something I realized I'd been missing for a very long time. A lightness of spirit. It was that feeling you get when you reconnect with an old friend after a long absence, when you try something new and it makes your feel alive, when you take a walk on the beach or a hike in the mountains on a perfect sunny day. It was like a weight had been taken off my shoulders, and I was infused with new energy. I responded by letting out a big, long, deep breath.

That feeling would return over and over again during my weeklong visit to the Center, but in those initial moments, I was taken in by tranquility of the environment. Gentle music played softly in the background, and the soothing smell of oils and burning candles permeated the place. As I looked around, I saw shelves full of books, tapestries hanging from the walls, and comfy seating decorated with lots of pillows. It was like entering someone's home rather than a wellness center. And then there were the people. Every single person I saw seemed to have a genuinely welcoming and contented smile on their face. The place just oozed positive, loving, nurturing energy. I immediately felt calmer than I had in a very long time and open to whatever experiences were coming my way. I wasn't entirely sure what I was going to learn there, but I had a gut feeling that I was in the right place and in the right hands to begin my healing.

My scheduled activities for the week included a one-on-one meeting with Chopra himself and another with Dr. David Simon, now-deceased cofounder of the Center. At first, I was nervous to meet these well-known and respected integrative physicians and tell them about my experiences, but they immediately made me feel comfortable and supported. They also designed for me a personalized program, which included a mix of modalities of meditation, yoga, lifestyle classes, and herbal supplements. Over the next week, I experienced a range of treatments and individual consultations that introduced me to the foundational teachings of the Chopra Center. I learned more about the mind-body connection while having Ayurvedic massages and body treatments. I learned about yoga, which I had never done, as a way to connect with my mind, body, and spirit all at once. And most importantly for me, I learned how to meditate. I had never meditated before, and it was a revelation for me.

The fact that I connected with meditation as strongly as I did came as a complete surprise. I had always been a type A personality, an active, even anxious person who really didn't like the whole idea of sitting still and doing nothing for an extended period. Nevertheless, I was interested in the idea of meditation in part because it made me feel more connected to my dad. I knew he had studied Transcendental Meditation back in the 1970s, and it had always struck me as kind of funny. My dad had been a bank executive who wore a suit and tie to work every day—not the type of person you typically associate with the practice of meditation, especially not in those days. But Dad had studied meditation as a way to relieve some of the stress and pressure of his hectic work life. And I figured if it worked for my dad, it was certainly worth a try for me.

So I did try. I was right to think it would be hard to sit quietly for an extended period of time. What I hadn't expected was that, even though it was difficult, it was also an immediate relief. After just one session, I already felt calmer and more grounded. By the end of my week at the Chopra Center, I was not just feeling more peaceful, I was also feeling more hopeful. Of course, not everyone will visit the Chopra Center, but what I learned there kick-started my return to life. That was my path, but there are so many different ways that we can all find the hope, energy, and inspiration we need to blaze a new path in our lives.

Choosing Your Own Path

Before I visited the Chopra Center, when I was first diagnosed with PTSD, I was heavily medicated for a time. When I was at my worst, the pills bridged a gap for me. My sleep medication helped me finally get some rest. My anxiety medication helped take the edge off. My antidepressants made getting out of bed in the mornings that much less of a struggle.

Overall, I started to feel a bit more functional—not back to my normal, functioning self, but like I was pointed in that direction. Once I got over the hump, however, the pills started working against me. They dulled my senses. They gave me regular headaches. I even developed restless leg syndrome. I was starting to feel like the medications I was taking, and the talk therapy that went with them, were more of a Band-Aid on my wounds and less of a permanent healing solution.

That feeling, however, seemed at odds with how my therapist was treating me. At first, he started me on a low dose of antianxiety medication. That helped to some degree, but I continued to have panic attacks, albeit less frequently. Every time I told him about another panic attack I'd had, he responded by upping the dosage of my medication. That, in turn, intensified the side effects I was having. It felt like I was stuck in a vicious cycle. At the same time, it seemed to me that if I was continuing to have panic attacks while on the medication, then clearly the medication was not treating the cause of those attacks.

Although I believe strongly that our culture turns to pills far too often as a quick and easy fix for all sorts of problems, I also want to be clear that I'm not knocking medication outright. When used in the right way, medication can be really helpful, even lifesaving for people, as it was for me—for a while. But after a time, I realized that the pills, even in combination with therapy, weren't going to bring about the kind of change I really longed for. That was when I started looking elsewhere for answers.

What the pills did do was allow me to dip my toe back in the pool of life again. Feeling more rested and a bit calmer, I started socializing more and engaging in activities that I had been avoiding. And that was what led me to the next step on my journey. That was what allowed me to open up to my friend and take his advice about visiting the Chopra Center.

The time I spent at the Chopra Center was a turning point for me. For the first time since my struggles began, it didn't feel like it had to be such a struggle to heal myself and get back to the person I wanted to be. That's not to say I was cured by the end of the week—far from it, and I still had a long journey ahead of me—but I finally felt like I had found a path I wanted to walk and some tools to help me along the way.

No matter what stage of the journey you're on, I think it's important to realize how unlikely it is that any one source will have all the answers any of us are looking for. There is no one-size-fits-all solution. No doctor, no guru, no spiritual teacher has it all figured out. There's no magical place to visit to find the answers. And that's okay. We all need to find our own path, and thanks to the fact that we're living in the Information Age and have the Internet and all sorts of different media to turn to, it's so much easier to do that than ever before. There is so much information out there that's easily accessible in the form of books, websites, blogs, that you don't have to spend a lot of time or money to go out and seek the sources of information and inspiration that work for you. You can visit places like the Chopra Center, like I did. Or you can go on a spiritual journey from your armchair if that's what suits you. Or you can do both.

As for me, I learned how to take my healing into my own hands by seeking out the kind of help I felt I needed at different times in my life. At first, that was therapy and medication. Then, it was the kind of help that the Chopra Center provided. My path would only expand from there.

The tools I'm offering throughout this book can help you determine if you're on the right path or if you need to make a change. When you slow down and start paying attention, you will find that your body and mind are giving you signals all the time about whether or not you're on the right track. If you feel like your current path or practice is ineffective or uninspiring, acknowledge that feeling, and decide it's time to look for new answers. That's all you need to do to start making a change.

My new path began with a nagging sense that there had to be a better way. I knew somewhere deep inside that the pills weren't enough anymore, and the side effects that went with them were too high a price to pay. I didn't know what I was going to do instead, but I knew I needed to do something. That thought alone was a powerful step. We don't always need to know where we're going before we decide to look for a new path. Trust the signals your body, mind, and spirit are sending you.

For many of us, when we feel things like pain, discomfort, or dissatisfaction with our lives, the natural inclination is turn away from that feeling, deny it, or ignore it. But that means we're ignoring the important messages that our inner beings are trying to send us. If it's time to seek a new path, there's no need to be anxious or frustrated. There's no need to turn away. Just say yes and accept the messages that your pain or other uncomfortable feelings are trying to communicate to you. And trust that the answers, if you're open to them, will find their way to you.

Going into Discovery Mode

My answers found their way to me because I opened up my mind and heart and started looking for them. When I had that life-changing conversation with my friend who knew Deepak Chopra, I chose to be open and honest. He was someone my husband and I knew through business dealings, so you might think he was the last sort of person who would end up helping me in this way. But that's what happens when we make the choice to open ourselves up to new possibilities—we start to find what we need. It just so happened that this person knew Chopra personally and that the Chopra Center was where the next stage of my journey began.

When I returned home, I was very diligent about keeping up my meditation practice. I was also inspired to learn even more about the ideas I'd been introduced to at the Center. I followed up by seeking out books by Chopra and David Simon and reading them voraciously. That led to me to more books by other authors on similar subjects. I discovered the work of Wayne Dyer. I became so absorbed by Debbie Ford's book, *Dark Side of the Light Chasers,* that I took her course on personal transformation in California. Both of these inspirational people have since passed away, and I consider myself incredibly lucky to have connected with them. At the time, I was like a kid in a candy store, fascinated by the new ideas I was being exposed to, eager to explore and uncover more. I couldn't get enough. The world was speaking to me in new ways, and I wanted to take in as much as I could.

Going into discovery mode and seeking wisdom and inspiration from new and different sources can be a positive, early step when you're still in the midst of suffering, or when you feel like the methods you're currently trying aren't working for you. It doesn't have to require a lot of effort on your part either. You can start by doing a search online or by picking up some new books to read. If you're feeling more adventurous, you can take a class on meditation, yoga, personal transformation, or something else you have wanted to explore. You may not connect with everything you try, but that's okay. If you keep searching, you will find what speaks to you. Simply doing things like this will also serve as a signal to yourself and to the world around you that you're open to finding a new path. And that can lead you to some pretty interesting places.

Several months after my first visit to the Chopra Center, another extraordinary opportunity came my way. Chopra and his friend Wayne Dyer had decided to lead a spiritual retreat to Egypt. They planned on taking a small group of people up the Nile by riverboat and end the journey at the pyramids in Giza, with lots of spiritual lessons and exploration along the way of course. When I heard about the trip, I jumped at the chance to go.

That was where I began to learn more about Dyer. (You don't have to travel as far as Egypt, but I highly recommend Dyer's work to anyone who is looking for new perspectives.) It was also where I deepened my meditation practice. I found that meditating as part of a group had a powerful effect on me. One cold night toward the end of the trip, a handful of my fellow travelers and I went together to the base of the Sphinx so we could meditate in its shadow. The experience of being in that historic locale while feeling all around me the supportive energy of people who were on a similar path, is something I will never forget. It was absolutely transformational.

Compare that to the state I was in just a few months earlier when getting out of bed felt like a challenge. I never would have imagined back then that I could be in such a place having such an experience. Anyone who has ever been brought to their knees by trauma or tragedy knows that life can take a turn for the worse in an instant—when you find out that a loved one died, when you get that cancer diagnosis, or whatever your personal experience might be. But it's empowering to remember that life can change for the better too. Real change takes time, work, and commitment, but it can also lead you to new places where you find yourself having amazing experiences that you never would have dreamed of before.

This was the stage of my journey when I was seeking and searching, when I was immersing myself in new ideas and absorbing everything I could. Not only can discovery mode be a powerful way to put yourself on a new path, but it can also be highly enjoyable and inspiring at the same time. We tend to think of change as difficult, as something we have to struggle to achieve, as something to fear. But the most important thing to understand about change is that it is the natural order of things. Change is constant and inevitable, so we might as well get comfortable with it. It's because we often fear change that too many of us stay too long in bad situations. But we can learn to see change in a whole new way, as something that doesn't have to be so bad, as something that doesn't need to be feared, as something that we can handle even if it sometimes makes us feel uneasy. And beyond that, sometimes it can even feel like a revelation.

Put Yourself in Discovery Mode

When you begin to see the world as a source of wisdom and power, then you will find that the answers you need are all around you—in the people you meet, the experiences you have, the places you go, whatever that might mean for you personally. Going into *discovery mode* is a great way to open yourself up to this way of thinking.

Start by *choosing three sources of discovery.* These could be books you read, classes you take, lectures you attend, or people you want to meet. When choosing your three sources, try not to judge them. You don't need to know exactly what they will do for you or where they will lead before you experience them. Just choose what you think will inspire you and open yourself to the possibility of finding new ways of thinking or being. And if you don't find them, simply keep looking.

If you don't know where to start, you can borrow some of my best sources. Looking into the work of Deepak Chopra, David Simon, Wayne Dyer, Debbie Ford, Brené Brown, Gabrielle Bernstein, Louise Hay, and Eckhart Tolle, to name just a few of my favorites (see the resource section at the end of this book for a more complete list) can be a powerful way to open up new paths that lead to new places.

Meditation as My Medication ... And So Much More

After meditating regularly for a while, I found myself waking up in the middle of the night with horrible night sweats. I consulted a doctor about this, and the conclusion we came to was that my body was trying to detox. I was still on antidepressants, which help produce more of the neurotransmitter serotonin in the brain. Meditation can also cause the body to produce more serotonin and oxytocin. My body was overloaded with these hormones, and the night sweats were its way of processing the excess and signaling to me that something was out of whack. After that, I weaned myself off the antidepressants under a doctor's supervision. My body gradually came back into balance, and my night sweats disappeared.

That was when I discovered that meditation could be my medication. I believe that much of the time, our bodies can serve as our own personal pharmacy. It was really through the regular practice of meditation that I found a long-term, sustainable way to treat my anxiety and depression. (That was what worked for me, but everyone's body is different of course, so please remember to consult your doctor before making any changes to your medications.)

As it turns out, those benefits aren't just anecdotal either. In the past several years, numerous studies have shown the positive effects of meditation on the mind and body. Remember all those negative side effects of being stressed out or stuck in fight or flight mode that I talked about in chapter 2? Meditation can basically serve as an antidote to all those nasty things.

When we're meditating, we're in a restful state, which is pretty much the opposite of the state we're in when we're stuck in fight or flight mode. A whole host of things starts happening in our bodies as a result. Our breathing slows down, and our blood pressure lowers. Our bodies produce fewer stress hormones, like cortisol, and more of what I call the "happy hormones," like serotonin and oxytocin. As a result, feelings of depression and anxiety are often reduced, and we generally feel better overall, no matter what state we were in when we started meditating.

Those are reasons enough to try meditating in my view, but they aren't the only benefits. We have all been exposed to so much information in recent years about the best ways to preserve our physical bodies, including messages about the importance of healthy eating, physical activity, and avoiding smoking, for example. However, even though we're living longer than ever before, we still hear very little about how best to preserve and care for our brains. As a result, people's bodies are outliving their brains more and more, and we're seeing a rise in cases of Alzheimer's and other forms of dementia. In the United States, it's estimated that one in three seniors will have some form of dementia at the time of their death, which is a pretty scary statistic.

There has been ample research to support the idea that meditation can help keep our brains in good working condition, just like exercise does for the body. Research published in 2015 by UCLA's School of Medicine shows that the brains of long-term meditators were better preserved than the brains nonmeditators. Everyone experiences some loss of volume in their brains as they age, but meditators experienced less, and not just in the areas of the brain that are typically associated with meditation, but throughout. Other studies have shown thanks to meditation the volume actually increases in areas of the brain associated with memory, learning, and the regulation of emotion. One of those areas is the hippocampus, which typically becomes damaged in the brains of people suffering from Alzheimer's disease. At the same time, brain activity and brain volume have been shown to decrease through meditation in the amygdala, the part of the brain that produces stress, anxiety, and fear. Being under stress has the opposite effect on this part of the brain. Chronic or prolonged stress can actually increase the size and the amount of connectivity in the amygdala and cause lasting changes in the brain's structure that negatively affects how it functions.

These are things that doctors never really explain to us, or at least none of my doctors ever has. If I had better understood what was happening to me when I was under so much stress, I believe I would have made different choices earlier on. That's why I think it's so important to seek out answers for ourselves, as the person most connected to our bodies, minds, and spirits, rather than just blindly taking the advice and pills that someone might prescribe to us. Keep asking questions until you really feel like you understand what's going on inside you. And if you're not getting the answers you need from your current doctors or advisors, consult more sources. There is so much information out there if you just look for it.

Meditation Is the New Black

Meditation's popularity is growing and growing, so much so that it has become a common practice among a wide variety of people, from celebrities to top athletes to veterans and school children. And for good reason. Here are some of the top research-based reasons why practically anyone can benefit from meditation!

1) **It Boosts Brain Function**

   Studies suggest that meditation can lead to better memory, focus, attention span, and much more.

2) **It Makes You Healthier**

   Meditation can make for a better body by reducing stress and inflammation and giving your immune system a boost.

3) **It's Good for Your Social Life**

   The practice can help lessen feelings of social anxiety while also increasing feelings of social connection and compassion for others.

4) **It Increases Positive Energy**

   Meditation can lead to an increase in positive emotions, feelings of satisfaction, and overall happiness ... and who wouldn't want that?

5) **It Decreases Negative Energy**

   It also helps tame the bad feelings, like anxiety, stress, and depression.

6) **It's Totally Doable**

   It only takes a few minutes a day to see the benefits. Even highly successful and super busy people like Oprah and Arianna Huffington can find the time, so next time you're thinking about zoning out in front of the TV or trolling Facebook, think about meditating for a few minutes first!

Leaning Into Discomfort

I have found another benefit to meditation that really helped me during that tumultuous time in my life. It was a chance to practice being quiet and still and staying in the present moment. I had gotten in the habit of being so reactive to the events in my life, fretting about the past and worrying about the future, and I had gotten out of the habit of being reflective and responsive to what was happening right now. Staying in the present moment and sitting quietly with oneself can be really difficult and uncomfortable, but one of the biggest gifts I've gotten from meditation is the ability to sit comfortably *with* discomfort.

That was a huge leap for me, as I think it is for most people. I had always tried to run away from or distract myself from uncomfortable feelings like fear, loneliness, uncertainty, jealousy, anger, and pain. I even tried medicating myself so I was numb to them. But those tactics only worked for so long. The bad feelings always came back. Early on, my therapist suggested to me that I "try to get comfortable with being uncomfortable." It sounded like a smart idea, but I had no idea how to pull it off. Until I started meditating.

Meditation helped me get comfortable with feeling uncomfortable because the more I allowed myself to feel the discomfort of just sitting with myself with no distractions, the more I internalized the idea that discomfort and difficulty weren't going to kill me and that bad feelings always pass. I was able to practice just sitting with my negative thoughts and, instead of trying to ignore or run away from them, allowing them to simply float by without paying them too much attention. Bad feelings lost their power in this way, and the effects of my practice spilled over into the rest of my life. It became easier to step back and think about what was happening to me in high-stress situations. It became easier to respond in a thoughtful way rather than flying off the handle. Not only did this lead to better decision making, but it also resulted in feeling happier and more at peace with the choices I made. And it was freeing. As the author and spiritual teacher Pema Chödrön once wrote, "This moving away from comfort and security, this stepping out into what is unknown, uncharted, and shaky—that's called liberation."

Of course, this took time; but if you are a type A personality like me, rest assured that meditation has been shown to have both long- and short-term benefits. Studies have revealed that after just a few weeks, or even a few days of meditating, many people already start to perceive a reduction in their levels of anxiety and stress, as well as an increase in focus, concentration, and memory. And if you can keep the practice going, those benefits will just magnify over time.

While I believe everyone's journey to heal and discover their true self will unfold in a unique and personal way, I also believe the tools I'm recommending in this book can be universally helpful. But if there is one tool that has helped me beyond all others, it is meditation. I felt the effects immediately, and those effects have only intensified over the years. I hope you'll give it a try so you can see how it might benefit you as well. It might even be a revelation for you, as it was for me.

YOUR BLISS TOOLBOX: MEDITATION

Meditation was a practice I first learned at the Chopra center after being diagnosed with PTSD. I was so churned up at the time that I needed a source of stillness, a quiet place so I could begin to make changes in my life. I think of my situation back then like that of someone who was stuck in a snow globe. At the time, my globe (my world) was so shaken up that all I could see was snow, not the pretty figures in the middle of the globe. I needed to calm down and let the air clear before I had a chance to do anything else. By calming myself and letting my globe sit unshaken for a while, the snow finally began to settle, and the figures in the center became clear.

So often, we look for peace outside of ourselves; but in meditation, when we get quiet, what we're doing is looking for peace within. That doesn't mean we try to *force* our minds to be quiet. Instead, we realize that the quiet is already there, underneath all the churned-up snow. We just need to rediscover it, and we do that by trusting the process and letting it happen when it happens.

The first time I sat down to meditate, I was tremendously uneasy. My thoughts were racing, and I couldn't stop them. This happened the first several times, in fact, but then I realized that nothing bad was going to happen as a result. My teachers assured me that I didn't need to judge what was happening to me. I was told I shouldn't have any expectations about my meditation experience because if it didn't live up to those expectations, it would only stress me out even more. In time, I would feel the effects I was looking for. Until then,

I just had to keep meditating because there is no such thing as a bad meditation.

This is the message I want you to keep at the forefront of your mind if you're trying meditation for the first time, or even if you have tried it before: *there is no such thing as a bad meditation*. It doesn't matter when you meditate, for how long, or what the experience is like—it's all good. Just trust the process and let whatever happens happen.

Basic Meditation Practice

Meditation is a great way to clear space in your mind for new wisdom to come in. It is also a great way to experience deep calm. There are different kinds of mediation, but the kind I'm recommending to you is a mantra-based meditation that I adapted from the Primordial Sound Meditation instruction I took at the Chopra Center.

Mantra means "mind vehicle" or "instrument of the mind" in Sanskrit. A mantra is a word or set of words that you focus your attention on during meditation. If you take a course in mantra-based meditation, you will usually be given your own personal mantra that you'll be asked to keep to yourself. But if you don't have a mantra of your own, you can use I am peace. With just that mantra and the following instructions, you can begin your own meditation practice.

Get Mentally Prepared

Throughout the day, we all have somewhere between 60,000 to 80,000 thoughts that run through our heads. When we first sit down to meditate, it can feel overwhelming when those thoughts come rushing in. A lot of people will be able to meditate for only a couple of minutes before the thoughts they would rather sweep under the carpet become too much for them to sit with. Some people get anxious. Some people freak out because they're not used to sitting quietly with uncomfortable thoughts; they're used to being able to distract themselves from them. Meditation can be really intimidating the first few times since most of us are not used to sitting with ourselves. So before you even begin, *take off the judgment hat*. Don't have any expectations for your practice. It may bring up some uncomfortable thoughts and feelings, but that's okay.

When they first take up meditation, people often say they just can't do it. To which I always reply, "You can't do it until you can do it." Don't get frustrated and don't expect to be an expert on the first try. It takes time and practice like anything else.

When you first sit down, thoughts may come in at a faster rate than ever before. Just remember that it will get easier over time. And keep trying.

Get Physically Prepared

Some people like to have incense or a special meditation cushion to sit on, but all you really need is a comfortable and quiet space. You will also need a timer to time your meditations. I like to use Insight Timer, an app on my cellphone, which not only tells me when my time is up, but also shows me how many people around the world are sitting down to meditate at the same time I am. I love thinking about meditation as something that a whole community of people is doing along with me rather than as a solitary experience.

I suggest that, to begin with, you start with just a five-minute meditation. Eventually, you'll want to be meditating for thirty minutes twice a day, but plan to work your way up to that. Think of it like taking your mind to the gym. If you're lifting weights, you don't start on the first day with fifty pounds in each hand. Instead, you start with maybe five pounds and add weight as you build muscle and get stronger. By the same token, if you want to take up running, you don't start by running a marathon. You start with a walk or a short sprint. Then, over time, you gradually increase the duration of your runs as your body gets stronger and more accustomed to it. Meditation should be introduced into your life in the same way. Start with five minutes on your timer and gradually add time as you feel more comfortable and you feel your mind muscle getting stronger (that is, less fidgety!).

Also remember to schedule times in your day to meditate. You may even want to put them in your calendar so you don't forget. You want to plan to meditate twice a day: once in the morning and once in the afternoon or evening.

The best time for your first daily meditation is first thing in the morning, as soon as you get out of bed, before any distractions can get in the way. This will also allow you to carry with you into your day those feelings of peace and calm that meditation brings. I think of it like diving into a swimming pool. When you get out of the pool and walk away, you're still wet and carry some of the pool water with you. The effects of meditation will cling to you for a while in the same way that water does.

For your second meditation, plan to do it after your workday or when most of your daily activities are done, but before you have dinner. Think of it as your time to wind down, your happy hour, only instead of winding down with a glass of wine or a beer, you'll be doing so through meditation. Then you can carry those feelings of peace and calm into the rest of your evening, just like you did after your morning meditation.

The Meditation

Once you're prepared, begin your meditation:

1) Sit comfortably in your chosen place and close your eyes. Sit up nice and tall in your chair or on the floor without letting your body be rigid. Keep your hands loose in your lap.
2) Begin by connecting to your breath. Become aware of how it comes in and out through your nose. Just observe how it changes, maybe getting faster, maybe getting slower at different times. Become aware of any sensations you are having in your body. Allow your body to relax by letting your shoulders sink, your neck and jaw soften, and so on.
3) You may become aware of thoughts racing in your mind. Never step into the traffic of those thoughts. Just stand on the curb and observe them as they come and go by. Don't judge them and don't engage them.

   You may also become aware of your emotions. Again, whatever feelings come up, you don't want to judge or engage them. Instead, let them float by as if they were clouds in the sky, just like you did with your thoughts. Then come back to your breath. Don't force your breath; just watch it. Eventually, it will spontaneously begin to slow down. As it does, notice how your mind begins to slow down as well.

4) Continue connecting to your breath for the first few moments. Once you're settled, silently begin to introduce the mantra "I am peace." Silently repeat to yourself: "I am peace … I am peace … I am peace." Don't force it; just let it flow naturally in whatever rhythm comes into your head.
5) Whenever you become aware that your thoughts have strayed, and you're no longer thinking the mantra, let the thoughts drift by and gently bring your awareness back to the mantra. Continue to silently repeat "I am peace" to yourself.

   Don't worry if you find your mind is still racing, if certain thoughts or feelings keep popping up, or if you're distracted by what's happening around you. This is all part of meditating, so just be gentle with yourself. The only thing you have to do is bring your mind back to your mantra whenever you notice you have drifted away from it.
6) Continue in this way until the timer goes off. After it goes off, don't just spring out of your meditation. Instead, release the mantra and take a few moments to sit quietly with your eyes closed and reconnect with your breath.
7) Close your practice by asking yourself, "What am I grateful for today?" This helps bring you into a positive mind space to end your practice.

Keep It Going

As I said before, start with two five-minute meditations a day, and then gradually work your way up to thirty minutes twice a day. It doesn't matter how long it takes you to work up to that point. Just keep going with it and continue adding as much time as you feel comfortable with until you reach thirty minutes.

It's important to continue with a spirit free from judgment, just letting each experience be what it is. But do try to make the practice a habit. Meditate twice a day, every day, and then pay attention to the changes that are taking place in your mind, body, and spirit. You will be amazed at what a difference thirty minutes can make!

CHAPTER FIVE

Failing Gladly

"Relationships are assignments for optimal growth and healing."

—Gabrielle Bernstein

Once you decide to take control of your journey, to seek your own answers, things are likely to start getting better for you. You may feel calmer. You may feel more empowered, like you are better able to handle things. Thankfully there are tools we can all rely on, including meditation and journaling, when we feel lost or overwhelmed. But we should also remember that feeling better doesn't mean it will be smooth sailing from that day forward. If we can keep this in mind and prepare ourselves, that's how we can guard against getting knocked off our true path in the future.

Deciding to take control of my journey didn't mean everything went perfectly for me either. In fact, I felt like my life was far from perfect when, about two years after Brittany was born, my marriage to her dad failed.

I've heard that when people experience trauma during a marriage, like we had with Brittany's birth and my father's death soon after, it usually goes one of two ways. The trauma can either bring the couple closer together, or it creates a rift that pushes them further apart. In our case, there was a rift that just kept getting wider and wider as time went on. After everything I'd been through, I really wanted someone to share it all with—both the joy of our new child and all the pain and worry about what came after. But I didn't feel like my husband was there for me. I felt alone. I no longer could do "alone" like I used to.

To be fair, Steve had been a workaholic for as long as I'd known him, and I'd been fine with that before. I was really the one who changed. It was an unexpected byproduct of the trauma and loss that I'd been through. As I started to recover from that and get stronger and clearer, I started to better understand my own needs and priorities. I was really longing for the kind of Brady Bunch–style family life I'd grown up with. My childhood home had always been filled with kids, and my parents were always around. But in my own home as an adult, most of the time, it was just Brittany and me since Steve worked late, traveled often, and was frequently distracted with the responsibilities of his job even when he was around. When I'd been growing up, my dad and mom were my biggest champions and supporters, always there when I needed help, advice, or encouragement. Now, with my dad gone, there was one less supportive presence in my life. I looked to Steve to fill the void, which wasn't really fair. No one was ever going to be able to make up for the loss of my dad. After a couple years, this dynamic took its toll on our marriage. What started as a rift grew into a chasm. We had just grown too far apart, so we decided it was time to go our separate ways.

It was the right thing to do for us, but in the aftermath, I felt like a complete failure. I had come from a family of intact parents. I was the youngest of four siblings, none of whom had ever been divorced. At the time, I didn't even have that many friends who had been divorced. I felt like I was all alone in this.

None of us gets married hoping to get divorced, of course. We all marry with the best of intentions. My intention was to recreate the Norman Rockwell, Hallmark-card image of a family that I'd had growing up. I wanted more children. I wanted a male role model like my dad. I believed in love and romance and happily ever after. When that illusion was shattered, it was like going into mourning all over again. I wasn't sure what I was going to do next.

Unfortunately, one of the things I did do next was get involved in another relationship that didn't serve me. I was vulnerable when I got into that relationship and even more vulnerable when I got out of it, so I then jumped into yet another, which eventually turned into my second marriage. It was a leap-before-looking situation, and not surprisingly, it also failed. In fact, my second marriage lasted less than a year.

And then there I was, about six years after Brittany's birth and my father's death, a twice-divorced single mother raising a child on my own. Somehow, everything I'd done to try to recreate the picture-postcard image of my family only took me further and further away from that ideal. It was heartbreaking.

And it was *embarrassing*. I didn't like this story about myself, and I hated the idea of telling it to my friends and acquaintances. But they were sure to find out. You can't hide a divorce from people, let alone two.

I used this quote from Deepak Chopra once before in this book, and I'll use it again now because it's a lesson that I think can take a long time to really get (I know it took me years): "Even when you think you have your life all mapped out, things happen that shape your destiny in ways you might never have imagined." The failure of those relationships certainly launched me onto a new path in life. It wasn't a path that I ever would have consciously chosen, but I now realize that my losses and failures were essential to my healing and growth, as they are for all of us.

My path to get to where I am today has been anything but a straight line. It's been full of ups and down, bends and circles, failures and mistakes. And so what if it has? Who among us doesn't have some detours along the way, some experiences that knock us off course? Even so, we can each choose to say that this has been *my* path, and it has led me here. As for me, I've discovered that *here* is a pretty good place to be, so it would really be unfair for me to regret any of it.

Redefining Failure

Have you ever wished you could have a "do over" or a "take two" in your life? A second chance to sidestep all the failures and correct all the mistakes? I think most of us have felt that way at one time or another, but it isn't a very useful way of thinking about our lives or about ourselves. Rather than regretting past hardships and judging your mistakes, have you ever thought that maybe you should consider embracing them?

We all fail at some point in our lives. In fact, if you really think about it, we all fail *a lot* in our lives. When you were little, you probably fell when you were learning how to walk, and then again when you were learning how to ride a bike. But then your parents picked you up, or you pulled yourself back up, and even though you were wobbly, you tried again. Eventually you learned to walk and you learned to ride. When you became an adult, the stakes got higher. You almost surely had a relationship that failed. You probably got turned down for a job or two or twenty. Maybe your child struggled in school, and you felt like you failed to prepare him. The exact details may vary from person to person, but no one's life is filled with successes alone.

How is it that we go so quickly and easily from "I failed at this" to "I'm a failure"? Why do we choose to define ourselves, and others, by the lowest moments in our lives rather than the triumphs? When my marriages failed, people from my past, acquaintances who knew little about what I'd been through, sat in judgment of my failures. What's worse is that I sat in judgment of myself. Why? My divorces are things that happened in my life, but they aren't who I am.

I've come to learn that there are really two ways to interpret past experiences. You can either let them inform and empower you, or you can regret them and let them disempower you. The important thing to remember is that you always have a choice. You can choose to focus on the negative, on everything that's gone wrong—which will only lead to more pain and suffering—or you can try to find the gift in everything that has happened, the opportunity to grow and change that comes from even the worst experiences.

I'm not saying it's easy to make that choice. So many of us judge ourselves harshly when we fail, so much so that we have developed a profound fear of failing. *What if I make the wrong choices? What if I screw it all up? What if it ends badly? What if I fail?!* Thoughts like these hold us back. They stop us from trying. They make us feel bad about ourselves. They stress us out. If you find thoughts like these popping into your head, then you should take a moment, breathe, and ask yourself, "So what if I do fail? What do I really have to fear?" Then you have to look at those past failures that made you so fearful and ask, "What have I learned from those experiences? Where would I be now if I hadn't learned those lessons?" With every obstacle that's put in front of us, we always have a choice to look at things differently. We can play the role of victim, or we can learn and grow, thanks to what happened.

We need to redefine failure. In the dictionary, *failure* is simply defined as "a lack of success," which doesn't sound like such a terrible thing. And yet, most of us attach all sorts of negative connotations to the word that don't really have to be there. We think a failure means we should never try again. We think it means people will laugh at us for thinking we could succeed. We think it means people will think less of us. We think it means we are unworthy. But, as the researcher and author Brené Brown said in her powerful book *Rising Strong*, "Just because we didn't measure up to some standard of achievement doesn't mean that we don't possess gifts and talents that only we can bring to the world. Just because someone failed to see the value in what we can create or achieve doesn't change its worth or ours." And, in fact, she goes on to say, "People who wade into discomfort and vulnerability and tell the truth about their stories are the real badasses." I couldn't agree more.

Failure, trauma, hardships: if these things that test us in life are also the things that most define who we are, it's important to choose to look at them in an entirely different way, one that is much more valuable and true. We can look at them as opportunities to learn and grow, as chances to better understand who we are and what we're made of. Pretty much anyone who has been successful at anything in life will tell you that failure has been part of their journey. That includes the likes of Abraham Lincoln, who ran for office multiple times, and was defeated multiple times, before being elected President; J. K. Rowling, whose manuscript for the first Harry Potter book was famously rejected by several publishers before the series went on to become one of the best-selling series of all time; and Thomas Edison who, in reference to all of his failed attempts to invent the light bulb, said, "I have not failed 10,000 times. I have not failed once. I have succeeded in proving that those 10,000 ways won't work. When I have eliminated the ways that will not work, I will find the way that will work." I could go on and on with this list of famous "failures" throughout history, but the point is, if you've failed, you're in excellent company.

That doesn't mean that failure isn't painful, but it's also an indispensable part of life. We need to learn how to differentiate failing at something, which is nothing to fear or be embarrassed about, from *being* a failure, which is simply a false narrative we tell ourselves far too often. Instead of focusing on the negatives, what if we chose to look at things differently?

What if we simply acknowledged from the start that perfection is impossible, that progress is not a straight line, and that ups and downs are what life is all about? What we're trying to do here is improve the overall quality of our lives. We're not trying to be perfect all the time. So let's be careful with the word "fail." Let's call it what it truly is: one of life's best and most valuable teachers.

Questions to Ask Yourself When You Think You've "Failed"

When failure or hardship happens, the question isn't "What's wrong me?" or "Why can't I do anything right"? The questions to ask yourself are these:

What did I learn? What did I learn about what I could do differently next time to succeed? What did I learn about who I am and what I want? What did I learn about my ability to pick myself up and try again? What did I learn about my own well of strength, resilience, and resourcefulness?

Where can I go from here? How can I take that experience and grow from it? How can I make my life better as a result of what I've learned?

These are the kinds of questions that matter most in life. How we react in such situations is really what defines us in life. So let's learn to define our experiences in a new way:

Failure = Learning experience
Trauma = Opportunity
Hardship = A gift we're given to help us see what we need to see, to emphasize what we need to learn.

Self-Love

I'm sure you've had a relationship (or a few) that you struggled with in the past—a bad break-up, a difficult divorce, a relationship you stayed in too long, or one in which you allowed yourself to be treated poorly. If we really think about it, we will all realize how much we have learned from our past relationships, even, or especially, the messiest ones. As Gabrielle Bernstein wrote in *Miracles Now*, "Relationships are assignments for optimal growth and healing." That was true for me. My relationships helped me see that I was looking for love and validation in all the wrong places. I had a hole inside of me, created by the loss of my dad and the traumas I'd suffered, but I was looking to the outside for something to fill it. I wanted someone to replace my dad. I wanted back those feelings of comfort, security, validation, and love that he had always given me. I thought I needed to find a man who could give me those things instead of finding a way to give them to myself.

The other thing I eventually realized was that I was making bad decisions about love because I had shut down my heart. After everything that had happened, I turned it off as a way of protecting myself from the pain. That left me in a place where I was making decisions about love from my head instead of from my heart, which, in retrospect, was not such a great idea. After the "failure" of my first marriage, I thought about what had been missing in that relationship and made a mental checklist of qualities to look for in another person. My second husband was an old friend, so he was connected to a past version of me that I was missing. He hadn't been married before and didn't have kids, so there were no complications of that kind. He wasn't a workaholic, quite the opposite in fact. His life was flexible and he was even willing to move from New York to Florida to be with Brittany and me. I had it all figured out in my head, and it made sense. I just forgot to ask my heart to weigh in. The truth was, I was never going to be able to fully love anyone, including myself, until I figured out how to open my heart again.

These weren't easy lessons to learn, and it took more than one so-called failure before I really understood them. I find it hard, even now, to admit how difficult it was for me, but that has been my journey, and I need to own it. So the question really becomes: How can I own my story but rewrite the ending? That's the same question we all need to ask ourselves when we are unhappy with our circumstances or feel like we've failed. My marriages didn't last, but that doesn't mean I no longer want that kind of loving relationship in my life. I don't believe that I can't have it or that I'm not worthy of it or that a relationship is not worth trying to have in the future. I want to choose for myself where to go from here rather than letting those experiences define me. We're all brought to our knees at some point in our lives. We will all inevitably find ourselves crumbling from loss and pain. So how do we push ourselves back up and incorporate those experiences into our lives without letting them define us? Because that's what matters most.

The answer is complicated, but it starts with love. Not love from someone else, which was the mistake I made, but love for ourselves. We need to know that, no matter what happens, we deserve another chance. We deserve to be happy. We deserve to live in joy. We deserve all these things, no matter who we are or what has happened in our pasts.

I know what you're thinking: easier said than done. And you're right. It's not easy. People often use the analogy of being on an airplane when the flight attendant says, "In the event of an emergency, put your own oxygen mask on first before helping others." I didn't do that. I wasn't focused on taking care of myself or my own needs. I wasn't trying to love myself when I was in the midst of suffering. I was just reacting to what was happening to me, doing whatever I could think of to keep my head above the waterline. I didn't even know enough to ask the right questions: Am I taking care of myself? Am I giving myself enough love to get me through this?

This is where learning how to access a quiet place within ourselves becomes so important. This is where the tools I've been offering you throughout this book will help. It's easy to say we need to love ourselves. It's easy to understand the truth in that statement. But at the end of the day, it can be very hard to do, even on the best days. And it can be especially hard when you're suffering. Self-love isn't just going to manifest itself in your life because you know it's important and you know that you need it. What we're talking about here is learning how to look at yourself and care for yourself in a whole new way. It takes practice.

It starts with the steps we've covered in this book so far—by understanding what's happening to you when you're suffering, by making a choice to live differently even if you don't yet know exactly how, and then by seeking a path that will take you in a new direction. All the while, you need to practice for the life you want. You need to practice slowing down your body and mind so you're not overburdened with stress and all its many effects. You need to practice connecting with your body and mind so you can better understand what you think and feel and what you really want. You need to practice sitting with pain and discomfort until you understand that it's not going to kill you, until you learn what it has to teach you, and how to help yourself feel better. It's in ways like these that you not only survive trauma and failure, but also begin to transform into something new and better as a result.

Limiting Beliefs and "What We Focus on Is What We Create"

Limiting beliefs are the things we tell ourselves that aren't really true, or that we don't yet have enough information about to know if they are true (like "I can't do it" … but how do you know until you try?), but that still guide our actions and decisions and can hold us back from living the life we truly want. In my relationships, the limiting belief I told myself was that I needed someone to save me, that I needed a man to make me feel safe and worthy. It took me a long time to realize that that was a false idea, that while I wanted a partner in life, I didn't need one to feel whole. I could find all those feelings of worthiness, security, and love that I needed inside of myself.

When we're afraid—afraid of failure, afraid we're unworthy, afraid we aren't enough—it tends to manifest as a haphazard array of thoughts, feelings, and limiting beliefs, a running dialog in our heads, a voice of judgment that says things like, "You're not good enough," "You don't deserve it," "You'll never succeed," or even "Who do you think you are?" In Buddhism, this is called "monkey mind," referring to the unstructured, restless chatter that can run through our heads. What I've come to learn about how our minds work is that when we're under stress, these kinds of negative thoughts become even more powerful. Stress affects our confidence and self-esteem, so when we're in a bad place, we're even more susceptible to negative thinking.

We have to understand that words hurt. We also have to understand that we spend more time with ourselves than we do with anyone else. We eat with ourselves, sleep with ourselves, spend all our time with ourselves, and we talk to ourselves in our heads more than we do with anyone else. We all know how much it can hurt when someone says something unkind to us, but how often do we stop to think about all the unkind things we say to ourselves? The silent words we speak to ourselves can hurt even worse. They can fracture our self-esteem, foster self-doubts, and rob us of peace, love, and bliss. Unfortunately, we can't get away from our brains when they're playing these kinds of hurtful messages on repeat. So how can we change the conversation?

What's in our minds matters, so we have to be better stewards or gatekeepers of our own thoughts. I always picture the classic angel-on-one-shoulder-and-devil-on-the-other image. As I've mentioned before, during the course of an average day, we all have somewhere between 60,000 to 80,000 thoughts going in and out of our heads (no wonder it's so easy to suffer from monkey mind!), and those thoughts can obviously be positive, negative, or neutral. It's important to learn how manage that barrage of thoughts, choosing to invite more commentary from the angel side, and shutting down the devil before he runs away with the conversation.

This is so important because what we focus on is what we create more of in our lives. It's like taking care of a garden. The more you tend to and water the plants and flowers, the more they will grow. It's the same with our thoughts. The more we focus on or "water" them, the more they grow and permeate our belief systems. That's true whether the thoughts we "water" are negative or positive, false or true, helpful or hurtful.

Every thought we have is literally creating our future. Every conversation we have with ourselves is overhead by every cell in our body, and those cells react according to how positive or negative the conversation is. If we choose to focus more on what's good in our lives, what we're capable of, and what we're thankful for (and we'll talk a lot more about the power of gratitude in chapter 7), then we can literally create more of these good things in our lives. But if we chose to focus on the negatives, the failures, the limiting beliefs, then they will come to define who we are and the kind of life we lead. As Henry Ford once famously said, "Whether you think you can, or you think you can't—you're right."

This is why it's so important to speak kindly and generously to ourselves. Focusing on the positive things that we want to create more of in our lives starts with something we have been talking about throughout this book: being aware or being mindful. You have to take time to slow down and notice your thoughts before you can start to manage them. As with anything else, this is something you can practice and get better at it. When you wake up in the morning, you can make it a habit to tell yourself that it's going to be a great day and that you deserve all the good things that are about to happen to you. And then, anytime throughout the day when you find yourself thinking that your job is awful, your relationship is terrible, and you're stuck in this lousy life because you're not good enough to make a better one, you can interrupt that conversation and turn it toward something positive. Buddha once wrote about the five factors that make for a "well-spoken, not ill-spoken" statement: "It is spoken at the right time. It is spoken in truth. It is spoken affectionately. It is spoken beneficially. It is spoken with a mind of good-will." The things we say to ourselves should follow the same prescription. The tools in the following section will provide you with more insight on how to do this, but it all starts with being more aware of your thoughts.

Having a positive conversation with yourself, one rooted in self-love, about what's happened to you is an important part of the healing process as well. After my marriages failed, I eventually learned to engage in some positive self-talk about those "failures." I started to tell myself that just because I failed at marriage didn't mean I couldn't get married again. I also looked back on my relationships and told myself that even though they ended, I was blessed to have had them. They taught me a lot about myself. I have Brittany as a result of one of them. And losing something doesn't mean it was never worth having in the first place.

Pema Chödrön wrote something on this subject in *When Things Fall Apart* that really resonated with me, which was, "Nothing ever goes away until it has taught us what we need to know." I believe the universe puts the same lesson in front of us until we learn, and that's what it did for me with my relationships. That's a gift. Being shaken awake may not be pleasant, but it is a gift. One of the most important steps in my journey was learning how to say thank you for the opportunities to learn. And now, I'm getting a chance to pass some of those lessons on to my daughter so she can be more aware and more prepared than I was. I tell her that I still believe in love, for me and for her. While I don't regret any of my past relationships, I now understand better now how important it is to be aware of what I bring to the table and what I want someone else to bring as well. And that was a lesson worth learning.

Your Bliss Toolbox: Exercising Your Mind Muscle

When we go to the gym, we train our bodies over time to be stronger, more flexible, and more responsive to stress. Well, we can do the same thing for our minds. We can practice stopping negative thoughts in their tracks and focusing instead on what we want to create more of in our lives. Over time, this will train our minds to be more aware and to see things differently, in a more positive, more beneficial, more blissful light.

Just like when you're starting a new exercise regimen, you want to start off slow and work your way up, doing these exercises more and more often. As always, remember to be kind to yourself and avoid judgment. If some of these practices are difficult at first, just know that the more you do them, the easier they will get.

Practice #1: Perform a Self-Check on Your Self-Talk

At any point during the day, you can stop and check in with how you're speaking to yourself by asking:

What am I thinking?
Do I like what I'm thinking?
Are these thoughts going to move me forward or get in my way?
Are the things I'm saying to myself meaner, less generous, more judgmental than I would say to someone else in the same situation? Or are they kinder, more generous, more forgiving?

You can also use Buddha's five factors of an "well-spoken, not ill-spoken" statement, which I talked about before, to assess how you're speaking to yourself. Ask yourself:

Is what I'm saying right now being said at the right time?
Is it the truth?
Am I speaking with affection?
Is it something that's beneficial to me?
Am I saying it in a spirit of good-will.

If you find yourself thinking negative thoughts, then consider how to replace them with more positive ones. "Think positive" can be tough advice to follow, especially when you're in a difficult place, but I find that an effective way to change the conversation is to ask yourself: What am I grateful for?

Negative chatter can start up in our heads without us even realizing it, so it's a good idea to practice this kind of self-check regularly to help interrupt that pattern. You might even set an alarm on your calendar to prompt you to do it at certain time each day. It doesn't need to take a lot of time. Just a few minutes will do.

Practice #2:
Get Out of Your Past and Your Future

The negative dialog we have about ourselves is often focused on either the past or the future. As I explained before, depression tends to lie in thoughts about the past—the "shoulda, coulda, woulda" thoughts—while anxiety lies in thoughts about the future, the unknown, or fear of what might happen.

When you notice these kinds of thoughts entering your head—"I never should have trusted that person" (past) or "I'm surely going to fail that test" (future)—an effective way to handle them is to do something that forces you to focus on the present. Anything that engages all five senses will help because it's really difficult for your mind to regret the past or worry about the future when it's concentrating on what's right in front of you.

One technique you can try is called the Chocolate Meditation, which is designed to help you engage each of the five senses: sight, touch, sound, smell, and taste. To try it, do the following:

1) Get a piece of wrapped chocolate.
2) Hold the chocolate in the palm of your hand and take a few moments to look at it, engaging your sense of sight. What does it look like?
3) Now close your eyes and roll it around in your hand, engaging your sense of touch. What does it feel like?
4) Next, with your eyes still closed, bring the piece of chocolate up to your ear and continue to roll it around in your hand, engaging your sense of sound.

While continuing to hold it up to your ear, use your other hand to slowly unwrap the piece of chocolate. What does it sound like?

5) Now hold the unwrapped chocolate up to your nose, engaging your sense of smell. What does it smell like?
6) Finally, place the piece of chocolate in your mouth. Hold it on your tongue for a moment and then being to chew, engaging your sense of taste. What does it taste like?

After you've finished your Chocolate Meditation, take a moment to monitor your thoughts by performing the self-check in practice #1. Ask yourself: Was I able to think about the past or the future while I was in the midst of the meditation? Are my thoughts more present after engaging with all five of my senses?

Practice #3:
Speak to the Child in You

If you have children, do you tell them regularly how much you love them? Do you tell them how special they are? What about when they do something wrong? Of course children make mistakes from time to time and do things to upset us, but when this happens, do you reject them or kick them to the curb as a result? Do you call them names like "screw-up" or "failure" and tell them how worthless they are as a result? Of course not. You're much more caring and understanding than that.

Think about the last time your child, or a child you know, failed at something or made a mistake. My guess is that you didn't respond by saying, "That was stupid. You can't do anything right. Why are you such a failure?" Instead, you probably helped the child to understand what happened and why, and you probably encouraged him or her to keep trying or to learn from the experience somehow.

Now, think about the last time you made a mistake or failed at something. Did you fall into the trap of negative self-talk? Did you say, "How could I be so stupid?" or "What's wrong with me?" If someone else said to you, "Wow, you're really a screw-up," did you internalize that message and repeat it to yourself?

Instead of letting those negative thoughts echo through your head, imagine for a moment that it was your childhood self who made that same mistake. Now think about what your adult self would say to that child. Would it be something like this: "It's okay, we all make mistakes. We don't have to deny them or feel bad about ourselves as a result. Instead, let's see what lesson we can take from this and how we can get past it."

That last part about getting past it and letting go is particularly important because fear, hurt, pain, judgment, jealousy, grief, loss, hate, revenge are the kinds of negative feelings that really weigh us down when we drag them along with us. The truth is that we are not our past mistakes. We are not our past pain. We are more likely to understand this about our children but not always about the adults in our lives, especially ourselves. We need to learn how to forgive people more readily—most of all ourselves.

Not only is this a kinder, more compassionate way to view ourselves when we've made a mistake or failed in some way, but it's also a more productive, effective, and empowering way. Life is not about how many times we fall. It's about how we pick ourselves up and how we *show up today*.

You can do this exercise to reframe the dialog inside your mind anytime you start to feel like a failure or find you have negative thoughts running through your head. Take out your journal and write down some of the thoughts you're having and why. Then stop for a moment, breathe, and take a new perspective. Imagine that child inside of you and write down what you'd say to that child in the same situation. Once you've finished, compare the two pieces of writing. I bet the second one will be very different.

Practice #4:
Kick the Inner Critic Out of Your Head

This practice has been adapted from a Creative Insight Journey course I took a number of years ago, and it's a way to help you put those negative thoughts in their place. To do this, you will need a blank piece of paper and some colored pencils or crayons to draw with. Then do the following:

1) Begin by thinking about those negative thoughts that sometimes run through your head. What might the person inside your head who is saying those things to you look like? This is your inner critic.
2) Now take a blank piece of paper and draw your critic. It doesn't matter if you don't know how to draw very well. A stick figure will do. But try to include as many details as you can: Is it man, woman, or monster? What does the face and hair look like? What shape is it? What color is it? What are its hands and feet doing?
3) Once you've finished drawing your inner critic, add three thought bubbles over its head. What is it saying to you? Write the words in those thought bubbles.

4) Now, give the critic a name. Its name should be something separate from your own name. Write its name across the bottom of the picture.
5) When you've finished, hang the picture of your inner critic where you will see it every day for the next week—perhaps on your bathroom mirror. When you wake up in the mornings, look at the picture and examine your inner critic. Read what it's telling you. Think about how those sentiments are getting in your way. Notice that the critic is now separate from and outside of you. It's no longer in your head.
6) After a week, tear up the picture and throw the pieces in the trash. You're inner critic is gone. You don't need it in your life. Reflect on the idea that you can chose not to listen to that inner critic. It doesn't have to rule your thoughts.
7) Finally, consider how your inner voice of wisdom might answer or replace your inner critic. The voice of wisdom is kind but honest. It doesn't blame, shame, or criticize like the critic does. Instead, it sees you clearly and is curious. It offers solutions, not judgments, when you have a problem or have made a mistake.

For example, your inner critic might say to you, "You're fat and ugly." You may indeed be carrying some extra weight and your voice of wisdom won't lie to you about it. Instead it will say something like, "You are a beautiful person who would be happier and healthier if you lost a few pounds. Let's look for some ways to work toward that goal and make it happen."

Not Today, Carl

One of my current students did the "kick the inner critic out of your head" exercise upon my suggestion, and here's how it worked for her.

"After I drew a picture of what my critic looked like, I named him Carl and hung him up on my refrigerator. After a few days, when something emotional came up, I started to hear his voice and I would say to him, 'Not today, Carl.' I began to realize that he didn't have to be in my head unless I gave him permission. He certainly didn't have to unpack his bags and live there. After a while, when Carl would appear in other people, I would recognize him and be able to say, 'That's just Carl rearing his ugly head.' Then I would say to him, 'Not today, Carl.'

"Once I understood what triggered Carl, he no longer had power over me. He still visits from time to time, but he's no longer allowed to unpack his bags and stay for any length of time."

CHAPTER SIX

When Life Gets in the Way

"Gratitude unlocks the fullness of life. It turns what we have into enough, and more. It turns denial into acceptance, chaos into order, confusion into clarity … It turns problems into gifts, failures into success, the unexpected into perfect timing, and mistakes into important events. Gratitude makes sense of our past, brings peace for today and creates a vision for tomorrow."

—Melody Beattie

About eight years after the back-to-back-to-back traumas that left me suffering from PTSD, I experienced a second brought-to-my-knees moment. At that point in my life, my first two marriages had failed. I was struggling, but I still held out hope of finding the right person to share my life and have more children with. Then I was diagnosed with early stage cervical cancer and that changed everything for me.

The problem was discovered during a routine pap smear. At first, it was just some abnormal cells that my doctor wanted to monitor. Then those abnormal cells progressed into *carcinoma in situ*, which meant early stage cancer in my cervix. As treatment, my doctor cauterized my cervix and continued to monitor me. Then the cancer cells began creeping upward. The bad news just didn't seem to have an end.

"You will need a hysterectomy," my doctor said to me when my test results came back showing the cancer cells had spread. It was a surgery that would remove my uterus and effectively put an end to my dream of having more children.

My hysterectomy had already been scheduled when I got another surprise. I'd been with a man for about six months, and we discovered I was pregnant. It was like some sort of cosmic gift, like the universe knew it was my last chance to have the child I wanted so badly, and in the eleventh hour it had decided to fulfill my dream before it was too late. My doctor agreed to postpone my hysterectomy until after the pregnancy, and we decided to get married. It looked like I was going to get my happy ending after all.

That was how I felt until my ninth week of my pregnancy when I suffered a miscarriage.

I was devastated. I was angry at my body for betraying me, first for getting cancer and then for messing up my last chance of having another child. I was angry at the world for giving me hope and then so cruelly and swiftly taking it away. I would never be able to have more children. The thought left me heartbroken.

On my doctor's advice, I went ahead with the hysterectomy, but even that didn't end things. About a year later, I had to have one of my ovaries removed.

Once again, it felt like the dominos of my life just kept falling, one after another after another. You know the feeling. Meanwhile, I was still planning to get married. I was in such a vulnerable state that it really wasn't the best time to be making that kind of major leap in my life. But I still desperately wanted someone to swoop in and rescue me, to be my knight in shining armor, ready to pick up the pieces of me and be by my side despite everything that had happened. So we went ahead with the marriage.

Like I said before, I believe the universe keeps putting the same lessons in our path until we're really, *really* ready to learn from them. My third husband carried with him one of those lessons that I still needed to learn. When you're encountering times like these in your own life, an empowering question you can always ask is: What do these circumstances have to teach me?

Out of the Frying Pan and into the Fire ... Once Again

I was starting to feel like I'd been here before. The old symptoms of stress, anxiety, and depression began to set in. I felt like I was careening through life, going from one crisis to another, just focused on getting through my prolonged health issues and managing an unhappy relationship with my husband. I was stuck in fight or flight mode once again. I wasn't able to focus on my own well-being or on living in bliss. Life was only about surviving from one day to the next.

That was the direction I was headed in when one day one of my closest friends suffered an emotional breakdown. Her husband had left her, without warning, for another woman at a time in her life when her son had recently left home and she wasn't working. She suddenly found herself completely alone, and she didn't know what to do. She felt like she no longer had any worth or purpose. She felt isolated, without anyone to turn to for support. It all became more than she could bear.

I think it was because I had been through my own periods of depression that I could see before others could that she was slipping further and further into that dark hole. Unless you've experienced mental illness yourself, I think it's hard to put yourself in the shoes of someone who's suffering from it. But I could. I knew I had to do something, so I was honest with her. I told her that I saw myself in her, that I recognized the signs of her struggle because I had been through them myself. I had needed help to dig myself out of that hole, and I told her that I thought she should get help too. She didn't protest. I think she knew in her heart how bad things really were even if she didn't know how to say it, what to do, or who to turn to get better.

I got her to see my therapist, who was concerned enough that he recommended my friend be hospitalized until she got over the worst of her depression. My friend decided against it. Soon after, she attempted suicide.

I got the call from her sister who told me there had been an accident. No one in the family was ready to admit the truth at that point, which was that she had tried to take an overdose of pills. She had passed out before she could finish swallowing the last of them, and her sister had found her lying on the bathroom floor. After that, she did get treatment in a rehabilitation facility, and she did get better. But it was still so hard for me to accept. Watching someone I cared about suffer so deeply was nearly as hard as suffering myself.

I felt that way again less than a year later when I got a call from my sister in Philadelphia. She left a message on my voice mail to call her back as soon as I could. I knew from the way she said it that she had something important to tell me, but I never expected anything like what I heard when I called her back.

"He's dead. Bradley's dead," my sister said to me. She and her husband, along with their daughter Tori, had been getting ready to drive from their home in Philadelphia to Massachusetts to spend Easter weekend with their son, Bradley, who was living there. Thursday afternoon, just before they planned to leave, they got the call. Bradley's heart had suddenly given out earlier that day due to an undetected heart condition.

It was all so confusing, so hard to grasp in the moment. There had been no warning. No one had seen this coming. After all, Bradley was only twenty-four years old. After I finished talking to my sister, I did just what I had done after I'd learned that my father had died. I went straight into "go mode." I started connecting with family members and helping to make arrangements. Two days later, I flew to Philadelphia so I could be there for my sister and her family.

In many ways the experience was similar to the last time my family had gathered together to mourn the loss of my dad. But it was different in some ways too. For one thing, I felt like

I had more compassion and empathy to share this time around. I took my sister and both her daughters out, one at a time, on a shopping trip to find something for them to wear to the funeral. They were still in shock, overwhelmed by sadness, and overburdened by all the decisions that have to be made after someone's passing, so when it came to the basic task of picking out an outfit, their minds just weren't working well. I was able to guide them and offer an opinion, while also getting a chance to talk to each one individually about memories of Bradley. Each member of his immediate family was planning on speaking at the funeral, so we talked about how they could each honor him in their own way. These were memorable moments for me, and I think for them as well.

After I returned home, however, the real fallout happened for me. Bradley's death on top of my friend's suicide attempt, on top of my ongoing health problems and failing marriage, were all just too much to bear. These events, stacked upon each other, served as a trigger for me, and I began replaying some of my earlier traumas. The familiar symptoms of PTSD started to creep back into my life bit by bit, and since I never seemed to have a break long enough to fully recover from one event before the next one hit, the symptoms just kept getting worse and worse.

The reality is that no matter how much work we've done on ourselves, life has a way of continuing to challenge us all. I think of it like a fast-pitch baseball machine. Life has a way of pitching balls at you again and again. You can't control the timing, the pace, or the angle of impact. But you can practice your swing so that you're in a better position to handle that ball the next time it comes. That's what I've learned to do over the years. I've learned to accept that I can't stop bad things from happening, but that doesn't mean I have no control over my life. I have a choice in how I view the events in my life, whether I focus on the bad or on the good. I have a choice in how I prepare myself to face and weather the storms that will come, because they always will. And I have a choice in how I treat and care for myself each and every day, no matter what life is throwing my way.

Getting Back On the Horse

In the years between my first brought-to-my-knees period and my second, I had gotten away from many of the things that had made a real difference and helped me recover the first time around. My regular meditation practice, for example, had become occasional, and I had lapsed into what I now call "crisis meditation" mode, which is when someone only remembers to meditate when the stuff hits the fan.

This time around, getting back on track was easier. Not easy, but easier. Thanks to all the work I'd done before, I wasn't starting from scratch. I went through a similar process to the one I described in chapter 4, only this time I had a starting place. Three basic things helped bring me back to the path I always wanted to walk in the first place and they can help you too:

1) Remind yourself why you wanted to change.
2) Reconnect with your sources of wisdom.
3) Reintroduce your bliss tools back into your life.

The first thing, reminding yourself why you want to change, has to do with finding the right motivation. When I asked myself why I wanted to change the first time, I had a baby to take care of. I didn't feel like I was capable of being there for Brittany in the way I wanted to, so that was my primary motivation for changing my life. This time my daughter was still a big motivator, but I also wanted to change things for myself. I no longer wanted to feel the way I'd been feeling, and I knew from past experience that I didn't have to.

Next, I reconnected with my sources of wisdom and inspiration. Previously, I had found a new path toward healing at the Chopra Center, so I decided to return to the source. The most powerful and affecting course that I had taken there was called Seduction of Spirit, so I decided to take it again. The focus of the course is on helping people discover who they really are and what their true purpose is. It was also a chance to get away from everything that was happening in my life and just focus on myself for a week.

Finally, I got back in touch with the tools that had helped bring me back to life in the first place. I resumed my meditation practice. I also returned to my journaling and breathing exercises. These tools can help us all be more mindful of what is happening to us as a result of what is going on in our lives. Once we have that awareness, then we can work on making changes bit by bit.

All the while, I reminded myself of what I had learned about being kind to myself. There was no reason to beat myself up because I had suffered a setback. (Remember: fail gladly!) It was a hard time for me, but looking back, I realize it was also an opportunity to renew my commitment to my practice and to taking care of myself. Any setback can serve the same positive purpose for you.

Show Up Differently

Any trauma can be seen as an opportunity to deal with things in a new way. There's a quote that I hung in a prominent place in my home because I like to look at it often, which says, "Life is not about waiting for the storm to pass but about learning how to dance in the rain." This is a wonderful thought to keep in mind when we're face with hard times. These are the experiences that allow us to practice showing up differently, which means approaching situations or people without expectations or judgment. We all have default patterns that we fall back on, especially when things get tough, but if we can interrupt those patterns and approach things differently, then we give ourselves an opportunity to grow.

This is something that we practice doing when we meditate. Every meditation is different, so when we sit down to start a new one, we are meant to have no expectations for the experience. And when thoughts or feelings flow in and out of us during meditation, we get to practice simply noticing them and then turning our focus back to the mantra instead of judging or trying to control them.

I've found that this is a useful way to approach life as well. Rather than fall back on default patterns, which we're conditioned to do when someone disappoints us or when we encounter the same old stresses, we can chose to switch to observer mode and let the situation unfold differently. For example, I was once talking to a friend who had just had an argument with her husband. When I asked her how she handled it, she told me, "I just walked away like I always do when he gets so angry about something."

I thought about that for a moment, and then I asked her, "What would happen if you didn't walk away next time?"

"What do you mean?" she asked me.

"Well, instead of doing the same thing that you always do in these situations, what if you stayed instead. What's the worst that could happen?"

She thought about that for a moment and really didn't have an answer. She didn't know why she always reacted the same way. She just did.

The point is that just because the conversation was going to be difficult or uncomfortable for her, it didn't mean she had to avoid it. Instead, she could choose to sit there with those feelings of discomfort and difficulty, and learn to live with them. After all, they weren't going to kill her. And after she got more comfortable with feeling that discomfort, maybe she and her husband could find a way to get past their anger and come to a resolution, rather than just repeating old patterns that left them feeling unhappy. One of the benefits of showing up differently is that it allows the people around you to show up differently as well. When you behave differently, it signals to others that they can do so as well.

The fallout I experienced after my cancer diagnosis was different than what I felt after Brittany's birth and my dad's death. I believe I was more comfortable with discomfort because of what I'd learned the first time around. Those earlier hardships allowed me to find my path out of the darkness more quickly and, as a result, I was thankful for the lessons they'd taught me. It can be hard not to look back on and regret difficult times, but part of showing up differently is choosing to see things in a different, more empowering way. Now, when I look back on the most difficult periods in my life, I'm not exactly happy about them but I do appreciate the path those experiences led me to. They helped me become the person I am today, and that's something I'm grateful for.

Consider Showing Up Differently

When you find yourself in a situation that makes you feel uncomfortable or that triggers you in one way or another, instead of falling back into old patterns of dealing with it, stop and ask yourself some questions:

What would happen if I didn't react the way I usually do in this situation? Would it kill me? Would something bad happen to me?

If not, then how might I handle this situation differently? How might I speak differently? How might I act differently? How might I react differently? If I were to show up differently in this situation, what effect might it have?

If there is someone else involved in the situation that's triggering you—if you're in a disagreement with someone, for example—instead of getting angry or walking way, try to get curious about where that person is coming from by asking, "Can you help me understand your point of view?"

After all, we all show up with our own points of view, and there is no wrong or right one most of the time, just different perspectives. Becoming curious about the other person's perspective is the best way to help you find common ground. It also makes it more likely that, in return, the other person will get curious about where you're coming from.

Practicing Gratitude

When I was helping my friend get through her nervous breakdown, I was reminded of something that I, too, had experienced when I was depressed. Many people don't really understand depression. They don't understand the death grip it can have on you. People will say things like, "You just have to get over it," or "Try to focus on the positive," without understanding how impossible that advice sounds to someone who is truly and profoundly suffering. Taking advice like that can be hard for someone who is simply having a bad day, let alone someone who is in the midst of a debilitating depression.

The one thing that did help me fight against the urge to sink into the dark feelings was practicing gratitude. Now, before I sit down to meditate each day, I take a moment to think about what I'm grateful for. (See the practice in the following section.) I also make an effort to practice gratitude anytime I find myself starting to focus on negative thoughts. I've found that this is the most effective way for me to shift my thinking, and I've seen it work for so many others as well. It's much easier than simply trying to "think positive."

A lot of research has been done in the past few years on the benefits of gratitude in a person's life. In fact, the University of California, Berkeley, has even established the Greater Good Science Center, which has as part of its mission to "expand the science and practice of gratitude." Studies there and by other researchers around the globe have found that the act of counting our blessings and expressing thanks to others is incredibly powerful. It has been linked to greater happiness, better health, and improved life satisfaction overall.

Among the hundreds of studies on the subject that the Greater Good Science Center has sponsored are ones that show the power of gratitude to help children, parents, romantic relationships, people suffering from depression, and much more. I even met a doctor through the Chopra Center who had been researching the effects of gratitude on heart failure patients. His name is Paul J. Mills, a professor of family medicine and public health at the University of California, San Diego, and a researcher of what he called "behavioral cardiology," meaning the relationship between psychological factors (good or bad) and cardiovascular disease. "We found that more gratitude in these patients was associated with better mood, better sleep, less fatigue, and lower levels of inflammatory biomarkers related to cardiac health," Mills explained. In other words, after just a few weeks of practicing gratitude, heart failure patients were better off in terms of both their mental *and* their physical well-being, which is a pretty extraordinary example of the power of gratitude, if you ask me.

What has been particularly interesting to me is the research that's been done on how gratitude affects people who are experiencing trauma. Not only do various studies suggest that in hard times it can help protect against PTSD by increasing a person's feelings of life satisfaction, but it may also help reverse or heal the negative psychological effects of having experienced a traumatic event in the past.

It may sound amazing that the simple act of focusing on what you're thankful for, instead of feeling sorry or bad about what you don't have, can have such a profound effect, but I've experienced it myself. Gratitude has been such an effective tool in my own healing that I even make a point of reminding myself to be thankful for the hard times I've been through, because of all I've learned as a result. It turns out that there is research to back up that view as well. The Kelly Clarkson lyric "what doesn't kill you makes you stronger" (from the song "Stronger") is more right than even she probably knew. A 2010 study published in the *Journal of Personality and Social Psychology* found that not only do hard times promote resilience and help us better handle future traumas, they also help us to better appreciate the good times in life. It seems to me that that's something to be very thankful for!

What Is Gratitude Exactly?

One of the world's leading scientific experts on gratitude, Robert Emmons, defines gratitude as have two key parts (described in his essay, "Why Gratitude Is Good"). He writes: "First, it's an affirmation of goodness. We affirm that there are good things in the world, gifts and benefits we've received."

The second part is to "recognize that the sources of this goodness are outside of ourselves ... . We acknowledge that other people—or even higher powers, if you're of a spiritual mindset—gave us many gifts, big and small, to help us achieve the goodness in our lives."

Your Bliss Toolbox: Gratitude

Gratitude means being appreciative, being thankful for what you have. Practicing gratitude can also be seen as another way to *exercise your mind muscle* (like we did at the end of chapter

5). You can choose to focus on what you don't have or what's bad in your life, or you can choose to focus on what's good, on what you have to be grateful for.

As with every tool in this book, gratitude is something that can be practiced no matter what sort of head space you're in. And the more you practice it, the more benefits you will see. You will almost surely find that the practice helps you cultivate a more positive and optimistic attitude and that it promotes a greater sense of life satisfaction overall. Beyond that, it can also help you face stressful and traumatic events that will ultimately come your way. It may even benefit your physical health. So why not give it a try!

Practice #1: Gratitude Meditation

You have probably already tried meditation and maybe even made it into a daily practice. Before you sit down to meditate, you can deepen the experience by asking yourself a key question: "What am I grateful for today?"

The answer can be anything, from the big things in life like my daughter or my home, to small things like a nice sunny day or the delicious meal I just ate. Sometimes I even tell myself I'm grateful for the meditation practice I'm about to engage in because of the peace and clarity it brings me. There are no right or wrong answers. Just ask yourself the question and see what comes to mind.

You can also pause and ask yourself "What am I grateful for?" throughout the day, anytime you want to change up a negative mind space. Sit quietly for a moment and then ask yourself the question. After you've answered it, notice whether focusing on the things you're thankful for has put you in a more positive frame of mind. I find that it works for me practically every time.

Practice #2: Gratitude Journaling

Journaling about what you're grateful for, or even keeping a separate journal dedicated entirely to writing about gratitude, is a great way to turn something like being thankful, which can feel a bit amorphous, into a concrete regular practice. It also gives you space to dwell and elaborate on the things you're thankful for in a way that just thinking about them may not.

You need nothing more than a blank book and a pen or pencil to start this practice. If you want, you can also find gratitude journals at your local or online bookstore, which offer directions, prompts, and inspirational quotes. The Greater Good Science Center even offers an online journal program (thnx4.org) with built-in reminders to be thankful.

Practice #3: Keep a Gratitude Jar

This is a fun and easy way to socialize gratitude and share it with others. I've done this with students in my meditation and yoga classes, but you can also do it at home, especially if you have young children in whom you want to encourage a sense of gratitude.

All you need is an empty jar and some scraps of paper or index cards. Ask the members of your family, or whatever group you're doing this with, to write down on a piece of paper what they are thankful for and then put it in the jar. Do this on a regular basis (weekly is a good place to start) until the jar is full. When it is, sit down as a family or group and read through the messages together. You might be surprised to find that the memory of feeling thankful in the past can be as powerful as feeling thankful in the present moment. In this way, you can feel even more thankful for what you've got!

CHAPTER SEVEN

Body in Balance

"Stress is like the laundry. It will always be there, and if you don't deal with it regularly, it gets out of control."

—Tara Stiles, yoga expert

"The bad news is you're standing on the edge of a cliff, and you're about ready to fall off," the doctor standing in front of me said with a mixture of gravity and concern. "The good news is that we caught you before you fell, and we're going to pull you away from the ledge."

We've all experience bad news coming out of nowhere. For me, this was a wake-up call. At that point in my life, my health issues, which began with my cervical cancer diagnosis, had been plaguing me off and on for eight years. First, I'd had treatment for the cervical cancer, followed by a hysterectomy, and then the removal of one ovary when the abnormal cells spread. Finally, my second ovary had to be removed, which put me into surgical menopause.

That was how I had ended up at this particular doctor's office. Dr. Michael Bauerschmidt is a functional medicine doctor, and I'd been referred to him for hormone replacement therapy since I no longer had ovaries to produce certain hormones naturally. Functional medicine was something I'd never heard of before, and my first appointment with him was an entirely new experience for me.

To begin with, Dr. Bauerschmidt spent a full ninety minutes with me. I was so used to being rushed in and out of examine rooms that I couldn't imagine what there was to talk about for so long. But Dr. Bauerschmidt had plenty of questions for me. He didn't just focus on the loss of my ovaries and my hormone levels, which were what had brought me to him. He wanted to know what else was happening in my life. He wanted to know about my stress levels, my energy levels, and what I did for fun. He asked about my mental health and my relationships. He asked about my diet, my exercise habits, and even my social life. He asked these questions, and then he really listened to the answers, making the visit feel more like a conversation than the rapid-fire interrogation I was used to getting from most doctors. He was warm and easygoing, but also authoritative and concerned. He had a good sense of humor, but also took everything I was saying seriously and to heart. It was like talking to a doctor, a therapist, and a family friend all wrapped into one. By the end of our first conversation, I already felt like I was in good hands even though he had yet to prescribe a single course of treatment.

After that, Dr. Bauerschmidt ordered a battery of tests. He checked my hormone levels and did blood work, which I'd been expecting. But then he also did a metals test and checked my adrenal glands. He did tests of my saliva, urine, and stool. Some of those tests I'd never had before. It was all part of his initial discovery process. He didn't just want to treat whatever symptoms I was having at the moment by giving me a pill. He was concerned with my total functioning (hence the term *functional medicine*) and how to help me function better over the long term. It was an amazing feeling to have a doctor look at me like that, like I was a whole person, instead of as just a collection of parts and pieces.

It was when Dr. Bauerschmidt had gotten back the results of all those tests that he looked at me and said those words: "You're standing on the edge of a cliff, and you're about ready to fall." It wasn't just my hormones that I needed to get back into balance. My adrenal glands were shot from years of stress and living in fight or flight mode. I'd been suffering the same old symptoms of PTSD that I'd had years earlier, including insomnia, anxiety, and depression. Dr. Bauerschmidt was the first person who took the time to peel back *all* the layers and see my entire situation. And he was the first doctor to do more than just prescribe medications to deal with what I was going through. He wanted to get to the root of my problems and solve them. What he was really prescribing was a radical change in the way I looked at and lived my life.

It was a pivotal point for me. I was being given another chance to bring myself back into balance and reclaim my life. Once again, I found myself at a point we're all familiar with, where we have to decide whether to sink or swim. I chose to swim, and I felt more confident than ever in that choice because I knew this doctor would be there to help me through it.

What Is Functional Medicine?

Functional medicine looks at the functioning of the whole person in mind, body, and spirit. According to the Institute for Functional Medicine (ifm.org), the definition is as follows:

"Functional medicine addresses the underlying causes of disease, using a systems-oriented approach and engaging both patient and practitioner in a therapeutic partnership. It is an evolution in the practice of medicine that better addresses the healthcare needs of the twenty-first century. Functional medicine addresses the whole person, not just an isolated set of symptoms. Functional medicine practitioners spend time with their patients, listening to their histories and looking at the interactions among genetic, environmental, and lifestyle factors that can influence long-term health and complex, chronic disease. In this way, functional medicine supports the unique expression of health and vitality for each individual."

If you're interested in finding a functional medicine doctor in your area, the institute provides an online list of practitioners who have trained with them. You can find it and more information at functionalmedicine.org.

Healthier Body, Healthier Mind and Spirit

After doing a physical examination and a battery of tests, Dr. Bauerschmidt came up with a treatment plan based on his thorough understanding of what was happening with me in body, mind, and spirit. The treatment started with intravenous supplements of the vitamins and minerals my body was lacking, and continued from there. It also focused on the basics. What was I eating? Was I getting enough exercise? Was I getting enough sleep? His theory was, if one part of my basic functioning was out of whack, then it would negatively impact everything else. That made a lot of sense to me, and it was a relief to be finally looking at what was happening to me in this kind of holistic way. After a few weeks, I started to really feel the all-around benefits.

You don't have to visit a functional medicine doctor as part of your journey, but it is a good idea to pay attention to the state of your body when you're going through trying times. Are you sleeping well? Are you eating well? Are you feeling ill? It's difficult for us to feel mentally and spiritually healthy when our bodies feel broken or burdened. The opposite is true as well. As my body began to get stronger, my mind and spirit started to feel stronger as well. I began to gain more confidence in myself as a result of feeling better physically. It also allowed me to see more clearly other parts of my life that were out of balance. That was when I started to examine more closely the relationship I was in.

It had been apparent for quite some time that my marriage was not a healthy one for either of us. There had always been a love-hard-fight-hard dynamic between us, which was at odds with the feelings of peace, stability, and well-being that I was bringing back into my life with the help of Dr. Bauerschmidt. It gradually became more and more apparent that I just couldn't maintain those feelings if I was in a relationship that didn't support them.

I knew my marriage was failing, and my husband did, too, but I was also afraid to let it go. I was afraid of what that said about me. I was afraid of what people would think of me. I was afraid of being alone once again, and that this time, maybe it would be for the rest of my life. Throughout the marriage, I had put aside my own wants and needs in favor of his. I had stopped living my own life, and I didn't know how to get back to it. I felt stuck. It was for all these reasons and more that I stayed in the marriage longer than I should have.

I had been hiding all this from those closest to me, compartmentalizing my life so that in public, I appeared outgoing, like I had it all. At home, however, it was like I was always doing and saying the wrong thing. I felt like I couldn't breathe. Despite my efforts to hide it, my family saw the toll the relationship was taking on me, and on Brittany as well. She and my third husband never really got along very well, which left her feeling uncomfortable in her own home and left me feeling stuck in the middle, trying unsuccessfully to make them both happy. My family assured me it was okay to get out. The therapist I was seeing gave me the same reassurances. But I still couldn't muster up the strength to pull the trigger until I finally started taking better care of myself. When I started to feel better, I finally could stop and say to myself, "I'm strong and empowered enough to put myself first and live my own truth."

Unfortunately, my marriage wasn't the only thing I lost during that period. As my divorce from my third husband went forward, my best friend of ten years decided to "divorce" me as well. Unlike with my husband, however, I didn't see this one coming. I was both confused and devastated by her decision. For a while, I was angry as well. It came as such a shock in fact that I'm really not sure which divorce was harder to take.

Eventually, I took the loss of both those relationships as another wake-up call in my life. I didn't like how I had been giving away my power, how I wasn't staying anchored in myself and making myself a priority in my own life. I realized that if I didn't like the person I'd become, then it was time to make some changes and stick to them. I also realized I had to figure out how to close the door on those relationships and move forward, even if I didn't entirely understand what had happened, as was the case with my best friend. How to accept those losses, mourn them, and then let go and move on to start a new chapter in my life was not an easy thing to do, but it was an important lesson that I needed to learn.

As I've said before, the universe has a way of putting lessons in our path as many times as we need to learn them fully. A third failed marriage and feeling abandoned by my best friend were certainly learning experiences for me. It was time for me to find peace once and for all. And in a way, those losses opened up new opportunities for me to do just that.

Feeling Out of Balance?

There are four basic questions to ask yourself when you're feeling out of balance:

1) What am I eating?
2) How am I sleeping?
3) Am I getting enough exercise?

4) What toxins are weighing me down?

For that last question, I mean any kind of toxin that could be keeping you from functioning at your best. When we hear that word, we're so used to thinking about environmental toxins or toxins in food—and you should definitely take note of those and do what you can about them if they are holding you back (by paying closer attention to what you put in your body, for example). But we often don't think as much about the emotional toxins in our lives, which can be just as damaging. If you're feeling out of balance, consider the thoughts you're having, the conversations going on in your head, the people you surround yourself with, and the stresses in your life. Think about whether any of these things are having a negative impact on you and ultimately getting in your way.

You've heard about the importance of all four of these things before, of course, but it can still be hard to get them right, especially when you're going through hard times. Often, one of the best things you can do for yourself if you're suffering is just focus on these basics for a while. The better you feel inside and out, the easier it will be to manage what's going on in your life.

Reconnecting Mind and Body

As I continued to follow the treatment plan Dr. Bauerschmidt had designed for me, I really focused on the basics of eating well, sleeping well, and exercising regularly to promote an all-around sense of well-being. One of the things that helped me the most during this period was yoga, and I believe it can be a transformative practice for just about anyone. It's one of the most effective tools I've found for keeping my body in balance. Practicing yoga helped me balance hormonally after the removal of my ovaries, and it contributed to my overall healing. Stepping onto my yoga mat each day also helped me connect spiritually, emotionally, and physically with myself.

Like with meditation, gratitude, and many of the other bliss tools in this book, there is a lot of scientific research that backs up the idea that practicing yoga has real, tangible benefits to our health and well-being. It has been shown to have a soothing effect on our sympathetic nervous system, which is the part of us that sends us into fight or flight mode during periods of stress. Yoga does this by reducing the levels of stress hormones in our system while simultaneously raising the levels of "happy hormones" like serotonin. As a result of practicing yoga, we are actually turning on our parasympathetic nervous systems, which is the part of us that is responsible for calm and peaceful feelings and less anxiety overall.

Further research suggests that yoga boosts the body's immune system, helping to protect us against illness and enhancing our ability to heal. It has also been shown to help the body manage pain. Of course, when I started doing yoga, I didn't know about any of this research, but I could feel the benefits almost immediately. My regular practice helped me feel less stressed and depressed, gave me more energy, and improved my overall sense of health and well-being. And I began to notice that I also felt the effect when I didn't do it: I just didn't have the same sense of balance in my body and mind when I skipped my practice, and the old symptoms of feeling stressed out would begin to creep in.

In one of my favorite books about yoga, *Slim Calm Sexy Yoga,* the author Tara Stiles writes: "Stress is like the laundry. It will always be there, and if you don't deal with it regularly, it gets out of control. Skip the laundry and the resulting mountain of dirty clothes makes it impossible to find anything to wear. Avoid dealing with stress and you develop a frazzled mind prone to outburst and meltdowns, making it impossible to deal with any challenge, from little bumps in the road to major life decisions."

Stiles goes on to say, "Of all the things yoga can do for you, chilling you out is probably the benefit that's easiest to grasp." That is a sentiment I wholeheartedly agree with. In the following section, you will find some of my favorite poses for "chilling you out," which I come back to again and again when I need to find calm and balance in my own life.

Your Bliss Toolbox: Yoga

The following yoga poses are some of my favorites for helping bring about a sense of calm, relaxation, and overall well-being. They are easy poses, and you should approach them with a sense of ease, not with the idea of doing as many reps in thirty seconds as you can, like you might do if you were lifting weights at the gym. These poses are meant to bring you back to center and help you unwind, so approach them with that intention in mind.

The following instructions will show you how to get into six simple poses that can be done anytime you want to feel more centered and relaxed. If you want or need an image to help you visualize each pose, a quick Google search of the pose's name will call up multiple pictures for you. Otherwise, you need nothing to practice these poses except your own body and a willingness to try. (A yoga mat is optional.) However, if you have any sort of health condition, including high blood pressure, heart disease, epilepsy, or glaucoma, please consult your physician before starting this or any new form of exercise.

Pose #1:
Child's Pose (Balasana)

This is a resting posture that helps quiet the mind and ease anxiety and stress. In it, you will be connecting your forehead to the Earth, so it's very grounding. It's also great for stretching your lower back.

1) Begin by kneeling on the floor. Your bottom should rest on your heels, and your knees can either be together or apart.
2) With your hips pressing back toward your heels, lean your torso forward so your stomach rests on your thighs. If it's difficult for you to rest in this position, you can pull your knees a bit wider apart.
3) Let your forehead rest against the floor. Reach your arms out in front of you, palms on the floor, or leave them at your side, palms facing upward—whichever is more comfortable for you.
4) Remain in this pose for five to ten breaths. Take big, deep inhales and let out the breath slowly. As you do, think about softening the muscles in your shoulders and hips.

Pose #2:
Standing Forward Bend (Uttanasana)

This pose helps open up and stretch the hamstrings, thighs, and hips. It's also an inversion pose, which means your head ends up below the heart, reversing the blood flow. Inversion poses are said to have all sorts of benefits to the body, including helping to improve circulation and lung function, enhancing brain function by allowing more blood to go to your brain, and of course relieving stress.

1) Stand with your feet about hip-width apart.
2) Relax your knees and bend at the waist, folding your torso over until your stomach rests on your thighs. If you need to, you can bend your knees a little so this is easier. Go as far as you can without pushing or hurting yourself.
3) Rest your palms on the ground or hold onto your calves, whichever is more comfortable.
4) Make sure your hips are forward, over your feet, and that your weight is evenly distributed between your two legs. Keep your neck soft and let your head just hang there. Remain in this pose for five to ten breaths.

Variation: With your hands, grab opposite elbows and sway from side to side a bit.

Pose #3:
Downward-Facing Dog (Adho Mukha Svanasana)

This is one of the most well-known poses in yoga. It's another inversion pose, so it provides all the benefits of the previous pose. It's also a great all-body stretch, working the muscles from your hands to your feet.

1) Start by getting down on the floor on your hands and knees. Your feet should be about hip-width apart, and your hands should be about shoulder-width apart.
2) Spread your fingers nice and wide. While pressing into the palms and finger pads of your hands, lift your knees off the floor. Gradually straighten your legs as much as you can while keeping your back straight. You're essentially trying to make a triangle with the floor.
3) Press the heels of your feet toward the floor. If your calf muscles are tight, causing your heels to be elevated off the floor, try moving your feet forward a bit, closer to your hands. You want to have as much of your feet resting on the floor as possible to keep you stable.
4) While holding this position, think about elongating through your spine and extending your tailbone toward the sky. Relax your shoulders and head, and make sure not to hold any tension in your neck. If your hamstrings are tight, you can soften your knees a bit.
5) Remain in this pose for five to ten breaths or for as long as feels comfortable to you.

Pose #4:
Seated Forward Bend (Paschimottanasana)

This is a great pose for stretching your hamstrings and lower back, as well as for helping the distracted mind unwind. It's also been suggested that it can aid digestion and help alleviate symptoms of PMS.

1) Sit on the floor with your legs extended straight out in front of you. Flex your feet so your toes point straight upward or back toward your face a bit.

2) As you inhale, raise your arms over your head. Reach toward the sky and lengthen your spine.
3) As you exhale, lower your arms and torso, bringing your forehead to your knees. Rest your torso on your thighs and reach for your toes with your hands. If you can't reach that far, rest your hands on your shins instead. You can also bend your knees a little if your hamstrings or lower back are tight.
4) Stay bent like this for five to ten breaths. On each exhale, try to sink deeper into the stretch.

Pose #5:

Legs up the Wall Pose (Viparita Karani)

This is one of my favorite poses to do before going to bed. I like to do it in combination with the left nostril breathing technique from chapter 2 to get myself good and relaxed for sleeping. It's also a great stretch for your legs and hips. As the name suggests, you can do this pose against a wall, but it also works in the middle of a room.

1) Start by lying flat on the floor. Then raise your legs straight up in the air, at a ninety-degree angle from the floor. Be careful not to strain your lower back.
2) If you're using a wall, your backside should be right up against it and your legs resting against the wall. If you're not using a wall, just raise your feet in the air directly above your hips. Your feet can be flat or flexed, depending on what feels better to you.
3) You can rest your hands on your stomach, lay your arms by your sides, or extend them straight out from your body like airplane wings, whatever is most comfortable for you.

4) Close your eyes and try to remain in this pose for about five minutes. As you lie there, become mindful of your breath. Try taking in deep breaths and letting out the air in long, slow exhales.

Pose #6: Corpse Pose (Shavasana)

This is one of the most relaxing yoga poses of all, but it can also be one of the hardest for some people because it's all about being quiet and still. When I have students do this pose in my classes, I often see them squirming about as they struggle to keep their bodies still. Just do the best you can. This pose is great for relaxing the whole body, lowering blood pressure, and fighting fatigue and headaches.

1) Lie on your back with your eyes closed.
2) Let your arms fall loosely at your sides with your palms facing upward.
3) Relax your legs, which should be about hip-width apart, and allow your feet to fall open.
4) Try to remain in this pose for five minutes. As you lie there, become mindful of your breath and allow your body to fall deeper into the floor with each exhale. You can also try the left nostril breathing technique from chapter 2 as you lie there to help stimulate your parasympathetic nervous system, which is associated with calming, peaceful feelings.

CHAPTER EIGHT

Giving Back

"The brain likes you to be a helpful person who is serving the world. The more you're thinking about service, the less time you're thinking about negative things that can make you depressed."

–Dr. Rudolph Tanzi

For those of us who are feeling mentally, physically, and/or spiritually unfulfilled, there is no quick-fix. It takes time for most of us to get into this state, so it will take time to get out of it. The state I was in when Dr. Bauerschmidt told me I was "standing on the edge of a cliff" had been many, many years in the making. So even though I started feeling better soon after beginning treatment, it was still going to take some time to fully heal myself in mind, body, and spirit. With Dr. Bauerschmidt's help, however, that kind of total healing was now my goal as I continued making regular visits to his office.

During my fourth visit, Dr. Bauerschmidt and I were discussing my depression when he made what I thought was an unusual suggestion coming from a medical doctor. He didn't prescribe me a pill or some kind of therapy. Instead, he said to me, "Why don't you start coming here to the office every day? Not for treatment, but to work. You can serve as the receptionist, answering the phones and greeting patients, and help with our marketing and client relations. That way you can be around supportive people on a regular basis, and you can learn more about how functional medicine really works."

The idea was immediately appealing to me. I wanted to get stronger. I wanted to be better educated. I wanted to be around like-minded people. And I wanted to feel better without resorting to more medications. So I agreed and started right away. I came in every morning and sat at his front desk, where I would talk to patients, make appointments, and do whatever I could to help the doctor and his nurses. It turned out to be exactly what I needed. Being depressed had made me feel so isolated and alone. Brittany was at school all day, and I spent a good deal of time—too much time—at home on my own. Having a reason to get up and out of the house each morning gave me a sense of purpose. And feeling useful, feeling like I was helping others in some small way, had a noticeably positive effect on my mood.

As my health and well-being continued to improve, some of Dr. Bauerschmidt's patients began to notice. I was looking healthier and happier, and when they checked in for their appointments, they would ask me about it. They wanted to know what had led to the transformation they were seeing before them, so quite informally, I started talking to people about what I'd been through and what had worked for me.

One of the first conversations I had was with a woman named Mary who was also going through menopause. She was having a really tough time managing her symptoms, which ranged from night sweats to insomnia to feeling edgy and out of it throughout the day. "It's hard to describe what it's like," she said to me. "I just don't feel like myself most of the time. It's like something has taken over my body and is keeping me from being me."

"I understand exactly what you mean," I reassured her, "because I've been there myself." I went on to tell her a little bit about all the symptoms I had been suffering after going into surgical menopause. She was surprised to learn that I'd been in a similar place just a couple of months before. "But you look so healthy," she said to me in disbelief.

At the time, I was feeling healthier overall, but to have that sense reflected back to me by someone I didn't really know meant a lot to me. It meant even more that Mary seemed to have a renewed sense of hope about her own situation after I described to her some of the things I'd done to get to this place. I was amazed that I could have that kind of effect on someone just by talking openly with them about all I'd been through.

I didn't know it at the time, but conversations like that one would lead me to a new path. Being part of a community of people who supported my healing and, just as importantly, whom I could support in return became an important part of my life going forward. I no longer felt isolated and alone despite all I'd been through. What's more, I found that, *because* of all I'd been through, I was in a unique position to really understand, empathize with, and even help people who were going through similar struggles. It had been a long time since I felt a new sense of purpose in my life, and that's something that we all need to feel whole.

From Student to Teacher

Dr. Bauerschmidt, too, noticed the changes that were taking place in me, as well as the effect I was having on some of his patients as I talked more and more openly about those changes. In addition to the treatments he had prescribed, which included things like supplements, nutrient IVs, biofeedback, and meditation, I was really trying to prioritize my health and well-being and make working on it an integral part of my daily lifestyle. I was exercising and doing yoga regularly, really paying attention to what I ate, and continuing the meditation practice I had first learned at the Chopra Center years before. I was faithfully sitting down to meditate twice a day, every day, no matter how hard it sometimes was to just sit quietly with myself.

One day after returning from the "Seduction of Spirit" retreat at the Chopra Center, I was talking with Dr. Bauerschmidt about meditation and what a difference it had made in my life. Of all the things I'd learned on my journey, how to sit quietly with my own thoughts had perhaps been both the most difficult and the most rewarding of them all. As I described to him how my meditation had affected me over time, Dr. Bauerschmidt had an idea. He had a speaking engagement planned for later that week where he would be talking to a group of people about functional medicine. "Why don't you come along," he suggested, "and talk to the group about how meditation has helped bring you back into balance. I think they'd be really interested to hear your story."

Of course I wanted to do it, but I knew it was going to be a challenge. I knew it would stretch me out of my comfort zone. Still, Dr. Bauerschmidt hadn't steered me wrong so far, so I agreed.

When we got to the event, Dr. Bauerschmidt spoke first. I was so focused on what I was going to say that I barely remember him speaking. After he was done, he introduced me, and I walked on stage. My anxiety immediately started to rise as I looked out at the stony-faced crowd staring back at me. But then I stepped up to the microphone and started speaking. I talked to that crowd just like I'd been talking to the individuals who came through Dr. Bauerschmidt's office looking for help and hope. The more I spoke, the more I realized how much I had to say. It was that day when I realized I really did have a story to tell.

That marked the beginning of my desire to teach. Dr. Bauerschmidt and I took our dog and pony show on the road after that, speaking at various venues, from large groups to a small class at my yoga studio. Everywhere we went the response was positive. People really seemed to connect with what I had to say and that just made me want to connect with people all the more. The idea gradually dawned on me that perhaps all the things I'd been through in my life had led me to this place. That all the traumas and suffering I'd been through had a purpose. That those experiences were what allowed me to really connect to people on a deep level.

Connecting with people was just the first step. After I'd earned their attention and trust, I realized I could actually help them. Everything I'd learned about my body and mind, all the tools I'd collected to help turn my own life around, could now be used to help others recover from their difficult experiences, find balance, and continue to care for themselves in a way that would lead to living a fuller life. I'd always wished I'd had a guide to tell me what to do when hard times hit. I realized I could be that guide for people. If when I shared my knowledge and my story, even one person didn't have to endure all the suffering I'd been through because I didn't understand what was happening to me and didn't have the tools to get through it, then that was surely a purpose worth having. The feeling of being able to provide help to someone who needs it, of being of service, is something that can uplift us all.

GUIDED BY PURPOSE

After that, I caught the bug. I wanted very much to teach and inspire people—just like the people who had taught and inspired me on my journey, such as Deepak Chopra, Wayne Dyer, Dr. Bauerschmidt, and many more. I had already gotten my certification to teach meditation sixteen years before. I hadn't used it much, but it was a start. Next, I decided to expand my credentials by getting certified to teach yoga. That way I would have even more knowledge to share.

The "problem" was I was forty-nine years old when I made this decision. When I went to my first teacher training class, I was one of the oldest people in the room. Even the teacher for teacher training was younger than I was. That was when those limiting beliefs, which I've talked about before, started to creep in.

"I'm too old for this."

"I'm not as flexible as everyone else here."

"I don't have as much energy as these young people."

"I'm never going to be able to do this."

Who among us has not heard those persistent, naysaying voices in our heads? I don't think any of us will ever be able to stop limiting thoughts like those from floating uninvited into our heads from time to time, no matter how much success we have in our lives. But what we can learn to do is notice what we're saying to ourselves and talk ourselves out of that place quickly and effectively. That was what I did this time around. Because I was in a more positive and mindful place in my life, because I had the tools, I was able to catch myself and turn things around before those thoughts stopped me from doing something that changed my life forever—becoming a teacher.

Instead of focusing on "I can't do this," I thought about why I was having thoughts like that in the first place. I didn't have to accept them as true, but I did become curious about where they came from. After thinking about it for a bit, I had to admit that completing this teacher training course might very well be harder for me than for many of the others in my class. After all, while I was in good shape, I *was* older, and I was also at a place in my life where I had more responsibilities at home than many of my classmates had, like having a child to take care of. But did that mean I couldn't do this? Just because it might be harder for me didn't mean it was impossible. Instead of giving up, I made a plan.

I believe in setting yourself up to win. It's something I talk to my daughter about all the time now. No one wants to feel like a failure, and feeling that way stops us from doing things we want to do. So when we want something in our lives, we have to ask ourselves what we can do to plan for our own success.

I started by setting myself a realistic, attainable, but also aspirational goal: I wanted to teach my first class as a certified yoga teacher before my fiftieth birthday. That gave me some time to get through the program, but it also meant I had to get started right away. I was well into my forty-ninth year at the time, so there was no time to waste! I also sat down with my daughter and enlisted her help and support. If I was going to be in class every day, then I needed to get some things lined up at home to make that possible. Together we mapped out a plan for how we would handle things like meals and transportation when I wouldn't be home as much.

Brittany became my biggest champion as I made my way through the program. All the while, I continually reminded myself why I wanted to do this: I really wanted to help people. That purpose kept me grounded and motivated until all my planning and efforts paid off. I finished my course well in advance of my goal, and I taught my first yoga class a full month before my fiftieth birthday.

The whole idea of becoming a wellness teacher and bliss coach just kept unfolding organically after that. I got certified as a Creative Insight Journey transformational coach, which is based on an empowerment course started by Dr. Michael Ray, originally as part of Stanford University's Creativity in Business curriculum. Eventually, I found ways to blend, together with my own experience, the different disciplines I had studied. Now I use a combination of body movement and mind practices to help people quiet their minds, relax their bodies, and safely examine their individual responses to stress so they can then make a shift into a state of balance, well-being, and ultimately, bliss.

Years before, when my own journey began, I never would have expected my life to end up in this place, but the more I taught, the more I felt like I was doing the right thing for me. As I connected with more and more people, and more and more people connected with me, I felt like I was coming into my own. I started to see how everything I'd been through had led me to become the person I am today. Those experiences gave me compassion for people. They were what inspired me to learn and understand more about how my body and brain worked. Those events shaped my destiny, and I remind myself regularly to stay grateful for that. Because without all the hardship, I never would have gotten to the place I'm in today. And it's a place where I'm very happy to be.

Serving Others

Becoming a teacher made me an even better student of how my mind, body, and spirit work together and what I can do to ensure I am functioning at my best. It made me want to learn about these things all the more, not only so I could help myself, but so I could impart what I'd learned to others. Over the coming years, I would continue to expose myself to experiences and people that would broaden my knowledge and allow me to have even more to share.

One such experience included a Journey into Higher Consciousness retreat to India that I was invited to participate in by the Chopra Foundation. The stated purpose of the retreat was to "connect people who, through personal and social transformation, are helping to create a more peaceful, just, sustainable, happier, and healthier world." It was attended by a fascinating mix of doctors, researchers, teachers, healers, thinkers, and more. It was there that I met Dr. Rudolph Tanzi, a Harvard Medical School professor and a leading expert on the causes of Alzheimer's. He and Deepak Chopra authored a book called *Super Brain,* which talks about how you can use your brain as a gateway for achieving health, happiness, and spiritual growth, as well as a follow-up book called *Super Gene*. During that trip, Dr. Tanzi talked to me about the importance of tools like meditation, exercise, and healthy eating for maximizing the brain's potential. He also talked about the benefits of being of service. "The brain likes you to be a helpful person who is serving the world," he told me. "The more you're thinking about service, the less you're thinking about negative things that can make you depressed."

Mahatma Gandhi once said something similar even though he didn't have Tanzi's research to back it up. He said (as quoted in *The Words of Gandhi,* edited by Richard Attenborough): "Consciously or unconsciously, every one of us does render some service or other. If we cultivate the habit of doing this service deliberately, our desire for service will steadily grow stronger, and will make not only for our own happiness but that of the world at large." I certainly found that to be true in my own life. The more I focused on helping others, the more my depression retreated, and the more my life—body, brain, and soul—got back into balance. It was another monumental shift in my life.

As I look back on that shift and ask myself why service has made such a difference in my overall sense of well-being, I've been able to break it down into a number of very powerful benefits. Here are some of the things that serving others can do for you:

Service reminds you that you're not alone. Starting from the very beginning, when I was simply helping out and interacting with patients in Dr. Bauerschmidt's office, I found that just being around like-minded and supportive people helped lift me out of my slump. Not feeling like I was alone in my struggles made a world of difference.

Service helps you manage your mind. When I was depressed and anxious, serving people helped get me out of my head, where I was focused on my own suffering, and into the world, where I could see that so many other people had been through hardships similar to my own. I talked before about how what we focus on is what we create more of in our lives. Serving others was a great way to shift my focus away from myself and what was "wrong" in my life, and toward being useful and helpful to others. It allowed me to really get out of my own way.

Service is empowering. When I first started speaking to groups alongside Dr. Bauerschmidt, I was amazed at the effect that feeling like I was helping people had on me. Depression, anxiety, and stress make us feel like we're at the mercy of forces bigger than ourselves. But even helping people in small ways made me feel empowered. If I could help other people, then I could certainly help myself. And the more I helped myself, the more I could help other people. It was an empowering cycle.

Service gives you a sense of purpose. I have come to believe that serving others is what we're all put on this planet to do. That can mean many things, of course, from being a good parent, to volunteering in your community, to making service your life's work, and so much more. All the tools in this book—which collectively allow you to slow down, get out of your head, and clear space in your life—can help you find what your unique purpose is and how you can serve others. Teaching others to find their bliss has become my life's true purpose. What's yours?

Your Bliss Toolbox: Serving Others

Because of all of the benefits I just outlined, I believe being of service is a crucial tool to add to your toolbox. But this doesn't mean you have to become a teacher like I did. There are all sorts of ways to serve others on a regular basis no matter what your profession happens to be or what sort of life you lead. You can do community or volunteer work, which can be anything from helping out at your child's school, to donating time at an animal shelter, to raising money for environmental or other causes. Or you can simply be more conscious of how you interact with people on a day-to-day basis and how you can make those interactions more positive. Following are some simple ways that you can start incorporating a spirit of service into your own life, or even enhance the spirit of service that you already have!

Technique #1: Meditate on the Idea of Service

Once you get a handle on your meditation practice, you can expand and enhance it by asking yourself some questions. Prior to the start of each one of my meditations, I sit down and take a moment to find some quiet before asking myself a series of questions that are important to who I am and how I want to live my life. Among those questions are: How can I help? How can I serve?

Sometimes ideas spring to mind immediately, and sometimes they don't; but asking myself those questions twice a day, every day, helps keep the idea of being of service top-of-mind in my life. It plants the seed. Because of that, I find myself looking for ways to serve in my everyday life, almost in spite of myself, no matter where I am or what I'm doing.

Technique #2:
Random Acts of Kindness

This simple idea has become something of a movement around the world in recent years. A random act of kindness can be anything really, from helping out a neighbor, to buying a stranger a cup of coffee, to letting someone who is late cut in front of you in line, to giving a gift. The amazing thing about this type of act is how instantly gratifying it is. You will be surprised at how good it makes you feel to make someone else's day a little better for no other reason than because you want to.

If you need inspiration, there are more suggestions in the resource section at the back of this book. The Internet is also full of stories about people who have committed random acts of kindness, and you can visit the Random Acts of Kindness Foundation at randomactsofkindness.org to find and share ideas. I suggest you put on your calendar as a regular appointment to make the first day of each month Random Act of Kindness Day. You can get even more out of this technique by finding a group of people you can do these acts with on a regular basis. You'll be amazed at how good you feel as a result.

Technique #3: **The Four As**

I first learned about the four As at the Chopra Center. During his lecture on the "Seduction of Spirit," Dr. Chopra spoke about how to awaken happiness and the four things that all human beings really need to achieve it. Those four things are:

Attention—to be listened to deeply by someone who is present and open to understanding our perspective, even when they don't agree with us.

Appreciation—to be valued for what is unique about us and to have that value expressed by others.

Affection—to be cared about deeply and to have that caring expressed through words, touch, and/or actions.

Acceptance—to feel like we are being completely seen and accepted for who we are, warts and all.

Focusing on these four As can make a big difference when we're interacting with the people in our lives. Even if serving others isn't a direct part of your job description or daily duties, even if you don't have time to be a volunteer, everyone has relationships that they maintain at home, at work, and in their communities. Enhancing the interactions you already have with the people in your life is an amazing way to serve. Much of the time, so many of us are on autopilot when we communicate, but if we make the effort to be a bit more intentional when we interact and focus on these four things that everyone wants and is searching for, then we really can improve our relationships and, in our own small way, make this world a better place.

CHAPTER NINE

Making Practice a Habit

"When we create peace and harmony and balance in our minds, we will find it in our lives."

—Louise Hay

My journey has been a long one. It was more than fifteen years between the time when I gave birth to my daughter, nearly losing us both, to the time when I became a teacher, helping others navigate their daily stresses and recover from the traumatic events in their own lives. It's a journey that I now look back on with gratitude, because it's brought me to a much better place. It's also a journey that I believe doesn't just end because I now know how to live in bliss.

As a teacher, I see a lot of what I call "crisis meditation" among my students. This is my term for people who learn meditation, but then don't keep up their practice. That is, until their lives get messy. When I see these crisis meditators return to my classroom on a regular basis, I know something has gone wrong for them. Whatever it is—sometimes it's an illness, sometimes a death in the family, sometimes a divorce or trouble at work, but it really can be anything—that's the thing that has motivated them to put the focus back on caring for themselves. They're suffering, they're in pain, and they're desperately searching for some way to feel better and restore balance in their lives.

I've been there. I don't judge these people, because I did the exact same thing at various points in my life. During the period after I recovered from the loss of my father and before I had to have the second of my ovaries removed, I was a crisis meditator too. I had basically dropped all the habits that had brought me back to life the first time around, so when I encountered this new set of traumas, I had to reintroduce them all back into my life. I had to learn the tools all over again.

I don't beat myself up for doing this. Not anymore. That's just the way my life unfolded, and the experience taught me a very valuable lesson. It taught me the importance of building a practice *before* I needed it. All my tools, from meditation to yoga to gratitude to being of service, were great for getting me through hard times. But what really changed things for me in a big way was when I stopped looking at these things as just a way to navigate trauma and started viewing them as an integral part of my everyday life. The pursuit of balance in body, mind, and spirit would no longer be an occasional thing prompted by some unfortunate event. It became a lifestyle, and that was when I really started to live in bliss.

When I talk to students about this idea of "building it before you need it," I liken it to dying a shirt a new color. If you've ever set out to dye a T-shirt, you know that dying fabric is typically done in layers. You might take a white shirt and place it in a bucket of yellow dye, for example. The first time you dip the shirt in the dye, it will have just a light stain on it. It might not even look exactly yellow when you take it out, but more like an off-white or a dingier version of the bright white shirt you had moments before. But then you dip the shirt in again. This time when you take it out, there's a bit more color on it. It may be the palest of yellows, but it's darker than it was before. Dip it in a third time, and when you take it out, it might be the color of straw. Keep dipping, and it will turn the shade of lemons. Dip all the more, and you can eventually get a dark, saturated yellow hue.

That's how I view the bliss tools that I've given you throughout this book. Every time you dip into them, you come out on the other side with a bit more color on you. And that color just keeps deepening and deepening the more you do them. And the deeper the color, the more prepared you'll be to live your life to the fullest—on good days and on bad ones.

That's why this last chapter is about turning the pursuit of bliss into a habit and making it a daily part of your life. Its aim is to help you develop a daily practice so that when troubled times come, you feel more empowered to handle them. But more than that, a daily practice can enhance the overall quality of your life, no matter what's happening. This is not just about trying to make the bad times better; it's about working to make the good times better too.

Whatever hard times have brought you to this book, try not to regret or lament them. As you move forward and create your daily practice, try instead to be thankful for those hard times because they are what brought you to a new path. Now it's time to let those events change you for the better. Let them lead you to a more balanced, more spiritually fulfilling, and more blissful life.

Spirituality Is an Inside Job

Stress, trauma, the hard times we experience in our lives, all leave an imprint on us. We can't stop difficult things from happening in our lives, and we can't stop those things from affecting us, but we can have some say over what sort of imprint they will leave on us.

Far too often, the difficult things that happen to us teach us the wrong lessons. We learn to close off our hearts when we experience heartbreak. We learn not to trust people when they let us down. We learn to be afraid to try when trying leads to failure. We learn to hide who we truly are when we get rejected, embarrassed, or mocked. These are common reactions, but they don't have to be the reactions we live with for the rest of our lives. We do have a say in the matter.

Instead, we can choose to respond to the events in our life in a different, more positive way. In one of the classes I took at the Chopra Center in Carlsbad, I learned about the seven ways that Deepak Chopra says people respond to what's happening in their lives and interact with the world around them. They are:

1) fight or flight response
2) reactive response
3) restful awareness response
4) intuitive response

5) creative response
6) visionary response
7) sacred response

These seven responses are like the rungs on a ladder, taking you toward a higher consciousness with each step. For example, we've already learned something about the fight or flight response, which is the most basic of human reactions and one that's not very healthy for us in the long run. It works when we're facing an emergency—like, "I have to get to the hospital *now*!"—but not for daily living. One step up from that is the reactive response, which is a state of being in which the ego attempts to manipulate and control situations in order to get what it wants. Chopra likens it to a child in a grocery store who sees a lollipop, and because she wants it, she takes it. This is an immature way of interacting with the world, one in which the person can't see beyond their own egotistical desires.

Ninety-nine percent of people in our society live in those first two stages of response. We learn those behaviors very early in our lives, and unless we do something to raise ourselves up the ladder, that is where we'll stay. The problem with these first two states is that they're not very positive ways of dealing with difficult events or with life in general. They ultimately cause more stress and bad feelings and leave us feeling unfulfilled. Sure, that child in us may get to eat that lollipop it wanted, but what happens when the lollipop is gone? We're just left wanting more and more things to fill the needs inside us.

So how do you break out of that cycle and move up the ladder? The tools I've given you throughout this book are a great place to start. It's through the daily practice of these tools—like meditation, yoga, mindful journaling, and the rest—that you can ultimately move out of a reactive state and into the restful awareness state, which is the third rung on the ladder. That's where you start to become more centered in your being and feel a greater sense of peace and self-acceptance. As you continue to climb up the ladder, it's like a waking-up process:

Level 4 is the intuitive response, which is characterized by insight, tolerance, empathy, and forgiveness.

Level 5 is the creative response, which is characterized by expanded creativity, intuition, and a sense of discovery.

Level 6 is the visionary response, which is characterized by a sense of service, compassion, and love for all people and all things.

That brings us to the seventh level, the highest level, which is the sacred response. This is what I call a state of bliss, but Chopra would describe it as feeling united with the divine. It is where he believes you can connect with God. By working our tools, finding that quiet space inside of us, and getting in touch with our true selves—that is how we can ultimately access the divine.

That is what I now strive for in my own life, each and every day. It's also what I hope this book is leading you toward. Life is about a whole lot more than just weathering crises and getting through hard times. All the tools and wisdom I've tried to impart up to this point will help you be more prepared for whatever comes your way. You will build up your immunity to hardship and become more equipped to manage life's ups and downs. But beyond that, I hope you will aim higher. I hope that once you recover and gain your footing, you will continue to climb the ladder so that you can have more joy, more peace, and be more in tune with your true self so that you too can experience the sacred, the divine in your own life.

You have everything you need to get there already inside of you. That's why I say that spirituality is an inside job. It's in you; you just have to learn to access it and cultivate it. And with time, practice, the right tools, and the right intention, you can and you will.

So what's stopping you? What would it mean to you to live a life in pursuit of that goal, each and every day? To live in bliss or in concert with the divine? Think about that question often and let it motivate and guide you on your journey.

Journal Prompt

Ask yourself:

> What would it mean to me to pursue a life of bliss, each and every day?
>
> What's stopping me from doing that?

Learning to Live in a Whole New Way

I discovered the path I've described to you throughout this book because I needed to recover from some truly traumatic events. One of the greatest discoveries of my life has been that I could aim higher than that. I could recover from what I'd been through and go on to live a life full of bliss. It has taken dedication and daily practice to get here, but now I can't imagine living any other way.

I now look back on my experiences and think about when I was first diagnosed with PTSD. I wanted to feel better right away, as many people do. I popped pills, hoping for a quick and easy fix. The reason why that method ultimately didn't work for me was because pills and other quick fixes don't offer sustainable results. And what I really wanted was a better life, not just to feel better for a while.

Another way of looking at it is to consider the levels or responses that Chopra says bring us closer to God. The pills didn't help move me up that ladder. I was stuck on level one, in fight or flight mode, and the pills just deadened my responses so I didn't feel it as much. Level 1 wasn't where I wanted to spend the rest of my life.

As adults, we have layers and layers of stories and experiences that color our lives. Whatever state you're in now, you didn't get there overnight. So when we find ourselves in place where we don't want to be, what makes us think we can get out of it overnight? It takes time to undo the effects of stress, heartbreak, loneliness, depression, anxiety, and shame. These things leave behind a residue that builds up in our minds and in our spirits. You can think about each of the tools in this book as a kind of cleaning and purifying agent. Over time, the daily practice of meditation, yoga, gratitude, and the rest will help clean that residue away. And then, without all that muck weighing you down, you can go on to choose the kind of life you truly want to lead, rather than being at the mercy of whatever events unfold.

Living as if You Have No Personal History

We need to rid ourselves of all negative residue in order to be our best selves. To climb higher on Chopra's ladder of the seven levels of response and not dwell on the bottom rung in fight or flight mode, we need to learn to unburden ourselves and leave some of the weight we carry with us. Otherwise, we're just too heavy to ascend.

What weight might we be carrying with us? The weight of our past mistakes, our past struggles, our past losses, our past regrets. We beat ourselves up over these things even though they're in the past and there's nothing we can do to change them now. What we can change is our future. What has happened to us in the past is not what matters. It's how we pick ourselves up and move forward that will define who we really are.

That's why it's so important to learn to release those past experiences, so that every day, when we get up, we can truly feel like it's a new day. Every day is a new chance to write our own stories.

Forgive yourself. Let go of the past. Focus on the fact that you deserve love and that you deserve to live in bliss. Because we all do. It isn't easy, I know, but it does get easier with practice. And you really have to ask yourself: What's the alternative? Holding on to past regrets, anger, resentment, is like drinking a bottle of poison and expecting the other person to die. One great way to break old patterns like these is to introduce new, more positive ones. And that's where establishing a daily practice comes in.

Meditation has been one of the most effective tools in my life for breaking old patterns. It has taken me out of that reactionary mode that I lived in so long, and helped me climb the ladder. Before meditation, I was like a hamster on a wheel, just going round and round and round again. When I meditated, I learned how to stop running in circles and just be—just be with myself no matter how uncomfortable that was. It helped me learn how to be an observer in my own life and take responsive action to what was happening in it, rather than just reacting in the moment.

The more you can find that quiet space where you can be an observer or a witness to your own life and your own self, the more you will come to know who you truly are. I talked before about how I now ask myself some questions before I sit down to meditate each day, like what I'm thankful for so that I can keep an attitude of gratitude about me. Some other questions that I've begun to ask myself are these: Who am I? Who do I really want to be?

We all get to choose who we want to be. Once we strip away the stress, leave the baggage behind, and put our egos away, that's when we can start to make this choice. We can begin to move from "this is who I want to be" to "this is who I am."

I could have continued living my life the way I had been living it in the past. I could have continued to beat myself up for my mistakes. I could have continued to regret my choices and the things I lost along the way. I could have continued to feel the pain of the traumas I'd been through. Dwelling on what's wrong in our lives rather than on what's right seems to be basic human nature, but that doesn't mean we have to let our minds get stuck there. I now consciously choose to focus on the positive, each and every day. When I ask myself who I am, I now answer by saying:

I am a mother.
I am a sister.
I am a daughter.
I am a friend.
I am love.
I am gratitude.
I am peace.
I am bliss.

My Challenge to You: Twenty-One Days to Bliss

If I can live in bliss, then I truly believe that you can too. It all starts with working your tools and making them a daily part of your life. These are the same tools that helped me on my journey, but beyond that, things like meditation, gratitude, and being of service are now medically endorsed. There have been all sorts of amazing scientific studies in the past several years, confirming their benefits and validating the work that people like Deepak Chopra have been talking about for more than thirty years. It's so cool to be teaching these ancient practices today, because they are so beneficial in today's world where people are more stressed out than ever!

Your Bliss Toolbox now contains seven key tools:

1) stop, drop, and breathe
2) mindful journaling
3) meditation

4) exercising your mind muscle
5) gratitude
6) yoga
7) serving others

To that, we're going to add the tool of a *daily practice*. The challenge I put to you is to focus on working these tools into your life in a meaningful way for the next twenty-one days, or three weeks, so that you can create that daily practice for yourself. Why twenty-one days? Because research shows that that's how long it takes to establish a habit or to break a habit. After twenty-one days, you'll be well on your way to turning practice into a habit that you can count on, day in and day out, to make things better every day, no matter what's happening in your life.

Your Bliss Toolbox: A Daily Practice

A daily practice will make every day better, not just the hard days (the opposite of "crisis meditation"). Here are some tips for making it happen.

Tip #1: **Rise, Shine, and Meditate!**

This is about starting your day off on the right foot. If you can do that, it will make the rest of the day that much better. When I teach people about meditation, one of the most common concerns I hear are these: "I just don't know how I'm going to manage to work this into my schedule every day." "What if I don't have time?" "What if I forget?"

We all have busy lives full of responsibilities pulling us in different directions. That's why I suggest you do your first meditation as soon as you wake up in the morning. This means doing it before having breakfast, before waking up the kids, before getting dressed, before brushing your teeth, before anything else. Get in the habit of waking up, maybe going to the bathroom, and then sitting down to meditate. Make this part of your morning routine, just like taking a shower, brushing your teeth, and flossing. In fact, you can think of meditation like mental flossing. You need to do it regularly to clean out the nooks and crannies of your brain.

The benefit of meditating first thing in the morning is that there is much less chance of things coming up that will get in the way. An even bigger benefit is that you then get to start off your day from a place of calm and balance rather than jumping right into the day's stressful activities. So many people jump out of bed when the alarm rings, immediately check their devices for new messages or news, and then rush through their morning routine so they can get out the door. When you start your day off like that, you're putting yourself in fight or flight mode before you've even left the house. But when you start your day off with a meditation instead, you get to carry that sense of peace, calm, and awareness into the rest of your day.

Tip #2:
Give Your Brain a Break

Even on good days, the plugged-in lifestyle that many of us lead can get in the way of bliss. The devices that so many of us have attached to our hips these days—our smartphones, tablets, laptops—can ring, ping, chime, or sing at us at any moment to alert us to new texts, emails, appointments, notifications, or what have you. That's why it's so important to intentionally plan times when you shut them all off so you don't always have to feel like you're living on the edge. Take away their power to interrupt you by choosing to shut your devices down for periods of time. I suggest doing this before going to bed, for example, and not turning them back on until *after* you've meditated in the morning. Make sure to turn them off before your evening meditation as well. It's also a great idea to plan other times throughout the day to turn everything off just to give your mind a rest. Put these times into your calendar so you can rely on having at least several periods of quiet time on any given day.

Think of it this way: We plug in those devices we rely on so highly each night so they can recharge and reboot. Well, people have the same needs. We all need to recharge and reboot ourselves on a regular basis. The only way the human body can start to repair itself on a cellular level is through meditation and sleep, so protect and prioritize those moments as much as you can. As author Anne Lamott once said, "Almost everything will work again if you unplug if for a few minutes … including you."

Tip #3:
Be the CEO of You!

You're the boss of your own life, the CEO of you, so give yourself the assignment of finding some time each day to dedicate to your own well-being. Make daily appointments with yourself and put them right into your calendar. Block off the time and maybe even set calendar reminders to practice journaling and meditating. This will help you make these things a priority in your life and help you establish good habits. At the end of this chapter, I've provided a sample calendar for working all the tools in your Bliss Toolbox into your daily life.

Tip #4:
Always Be Grateful for What You Can Do

This isn't about being perfect; it's about striving for change and doing the best you can, each and every day. That means reorienting your mind so you see each day as a new opportunity while never beating yourself up for missing an opportunity. After all, life doesn't always go exactly as planned, but that's okay. If you miss a meditation one morning, simply try again that afternoon and again the day after. And then remember to take some time each day to be grateful for the things you *can do* to live a more bliss-filled life. Focus on the *can dos*, not the can'ts or didn'ts, because the can dos are the things that matter most.

Tip #5:
Notice the Change

Take some time each week to be mindful and notice what effect using your bliss tools on a regular basis has had on you. Are you calmer? More peaceful? Less stressed? More present with your family and friends? This is a great thing to journal about at the end of each week. By the same token, notice what happens when you skip your daily practice. Note the changes in the way you feel physically and emotionally, in your mood and your state of mind. Remember, when we're mindful of what's happening to us, we can use that information to make better, more informed choices.

Journal Prompt for Noticing Change

Think about the last time you skipped your practice and then answer the following questions in your journal: What changes did you notice in yourself as a result of skipping your practice? How did it make you feel? What did you miss about your practice?

Now think about how you feel when you don't skip your practice. How are you different than when you don't use your bliss tools? How do you feel? How does it affect the way you interact with people? How does it affect your life in general?

Tip #6:
Reward Yourself

After you've completed your twenty-one days to bliss, take some time to celebrate! It doesn't matter whether it was a perfect twenty-one days; it's still something to celebrate. Take yourself out to dinner or buy yourself a small gift to mark the occasion. You deserve to live a more healthy, centered, peaceful, and blissful life, so any progress toward that goal is worth celebrating!

Sample Daily Plan

7:00 a.m.	✔ Start your day off right: Rise, shine, and *meditate*!
7:30 a.m.	✔ Spend a few minutes *journaling*.
	✔ In your journal, include a *gratitude* list of what you're thankful for on this day.
	✔ Eat a healthy breakfast.
8:15 a.m.	✔ Spend some time moving each day by taking an exercise class, going for a run or a swim, or even just taking a walk. If you're a morning exerciser, do this right after breakfast. If not, save it until the afternoon.
Midday:	✔ Perform some *breathing* exercises to slow yourself down.
	✔ *Exercise your mind muscle* by performing a self-check-in on your thoughts.
	✔ If you need to change the trajectory of your day, perform another mind muscle exercise from chapter 5. (For example: the "speak to the child in you" exercise or "kick the inner critic out of your head" exercise).
6:00 p.m.	✔ Spend some time moving each day by taking an exercise class, going for a run or a swim, or even just taking a walk. If you aren't a morning exerciser, do this before winding down for the day, before you meditate, and then enjoy a healthy dinner.
7:00 p.m.	✔ Enjoy happy hour and unwind from the day's activities, but without that glass of wine. *Meditate* instead!
	✔ Eat a healthy dinner.
10:00 p.m.	✔ Do your *yoga* stretches to relax yourself before bed.
	✔ While in leg-up-the-wall pose, perform the left nostril breathing exercise to calm your nervous system.
	✔ *Exercise your mind muscle* and replay your day by performing the recapitulation of your day exercise (see chart over page).
	✔ Get a good nights sleep.

Recapitulation of Your Day Exercise

To recapitulate means "to restate briefly," and that's what this exercise is meant to do: to help you restate briefly the events of your day. The idea is to replay your day in your mind as if you were watching a minimovie. Don't dwell on any particular moment or judge the events that happened. Just replay them, from the moment you got up to the morning to the present moment.

The purpose of this exercise is to help you process what has happened to you throughout your day. By reviewing the events as dispassionately as possible, you will be able to release some of your feelings about what happened during your day. That way you can go to sleep peacefully at night and then start your next day with less baggage to carry with you.

Day 1 Daily Plan *Be of Service* by committing one random act of kindness	**Day 2** Daily Plan	**Day 3** Daily Plan	**Day 4** Daily Plan	**Day 5** Daily Plan	**Day 6** Daily Plan	**Day 7** Daily Plan Take a *yoga* or other exercise class
Day 8 Daily Plan Volunteer or find another way to *be of service*	**Day 9** Daily Plan	**Day 10** Daily Plan	**Day 11** Daily Plan	**Day 12** Daily Plan	**Day 13** Daily Plan	**Day 14** Daily Plan Take a *yoga* or other exercise class
Day 15 Daily Plan Take note of how far you've come in establishing new bliss-filled habits!	**Day 16** Daily Plan	**Day 17** Daily Plan	**Day 18** Daily Plan	**Day 19** Daily Plan	**Day 20** Daily Plan	**Day 21** Daily Plan Take a *yoga* or other exercise class. Reward yourself for creating a great new habit!

EPILOGUE

Writing Your Own Story

The book you are holding in your hands right now is my story. I wanted to share it because I believe that when any of us do, it not only helps us heal, but it helps others heal as well. I hope it's been both useful and inspiring to read, because now I'd like to invite you to write your own story. Not literally (although I think writing can be a powerful tool for healing) but metaphorically. We are all the authors of our own life stories, so it's time to ask yourself: Where do I want my story to go from here?

If someone had told me years ago, when I was in the midst of suffering, that I would one day be teaching others and help them by telling my story, I would have said they were crazy. I was in no position to do anything like that at the time. I could barely help myself and my daughter, so how could I possibly help anyone else? I couldn't see past what was right in front of me. I couldn't see how much possibility lay ahead of me in the future. I couldn't see all that I might become.

But then, one thing led to another. A visit to a functional medicine doctor led to my working for him. Working for him led to talking to his patients about what I was going through, which led to the doctor inviting me to do speaking engagements with him. That led to me getting the teaching bug and deciding to train to be a certified yoga instructor. Starting to teach spurred me to learn even more so I'd have more wisdom to share, which led to Gabby Bernstein's books, then her workshop, which led to me wanting to find purpose in my pain and write a book of my own. And so on and so on. Some might call this a chain of coincidences, but as my mentor, Deepak Chopra, once wrote, "Coincidences are not accidents but signals from the universe which can guide us toward our true destiny." I've learned from him, and from personal experience, just how important it is to pay attention to and appreciate life's coincidences in order to open up a new world of possibilities. Chopra even has a term for this, "synchrodestiny," which he describes as a state in which "it becomes possible to achieve the spontaneous fulfillment of our every desire.

It was in this way, step by step, coincidence after coincidence, that I changed the trajectory of my life. I interrupted the broken record of negative thoughts playing over and over in my head, telling me that life would never get any better, and I started singing a new tune. I put down the weighty baggage of my past experiences, past struggles, past mistakes, and left it behind me as I walked forward on a new path. When you're stuck in a difficult place—stressed out, depressed, anxious, upset, suffering—it's hard to imagine that life can be any different than what you're experiencing right now. It's hard to see the other side. I know that because I've lived it. But that's also why I know that the other side is out there, and you can get there. I know that real, lasting, positive change is possible. I know it because I've experienced it for myself, time and time again.

If there is one final thought I want to leave you with, it's this: you really can change your life. If I can do it, you can too. You can survive whatever it is you're going through, and you can go on to thrive, just like I did. You really can have bliss in your life.

So what do you need to do to start writing a new chapter of your story, one that has a much happier, much more fulfilling, much more blissful ending? You don't need much. You just need the right intention, a little belief, and some tools that will help you pick yourself up when you're down and propel you forward. And then, you simply go—and keep going—from there. Pay attention to the coincidences you encounter along the way and where they might be leading you. When all else fails, return to your tools. At any given time, they are what will help you settle your mind and body, find quiet and peace, and ultimately rediscover who you are and, even more importantly, who you could be.

I never imagined I would be sharing my story in this way. I never imagined I would end up in a place like this. I never imagined that I could feel this way—so empowered, so purposeful, so at peace. But now that I've experienced it, I can't get enough. And I hope it will be the same for you.

May the days ahead of you be filled with balance and bliss!

Resources

If you ever find yourself at a point in your life when you don't know what to do next to make the kind of change you want or to find the answers that you're seeking, consider returning to the tools at the end of each chapter in this book or making use of the resources in this section to help you.

Sources of Information and Inspiration

Following are lists of sources cited in this book, as well as some additional resources that might be useful on your journey.

Books

This is only a random sampling of some of my current favorites. There are many more options, by these and other authors, available online or in your local bookstore. Any of these books, however, are a great place to start if you're looking for some inspiration to start making real changes in your life.

Melody Beattie

The Language of Letting Go: Daily Meditations for Codependents

Gabrielle Bernstein

May Cause Miracles: A 40-Day Guidebook of Subtle Shifts for Radical Change and Unlimited Happiness

Miracles Now: 108 Life-Changing Tools for Less Stress, More Flow, and Finding Your True Purpose

Spirit Junkie: A Radical Road to Self-Love and Miracles

Brené Brown

Daring Greatly: How the Courage to Be Vulnerable Transforms the Way We Live, Love, Parent, and Lead

The Gifts of Imperfection: Let Go of Who You Think You're Supposed to Be and Embrace Who You Are

Rising Strong: The Reckoning, The Rumble, The Revolution

Pema Chödrön

When Things Fall Apart: Heart Advice for Difficult Times

Deepak Chopra

A prolific writer with so many great books to his name; you can't go wrong by picking up any of them. But just to name a few:

Ageless Body, Timeless Mind: The Quantum Alternative to Growing Old

How to Know GOD: The Soul's Journey into the Mystery of Mysteries

The Seven Spiritual Laws of Success: A Practical Guide to the Fulfillment of Your Dreams

Spiritual Solutions: Answers to Life's Greatest Challenges
The Spontaneous Fulfillment of Desire: Harnessing the Infinite Power of Coincidence

Deepak Chopra and Rudolph E. Tanzi
Super Brain: Unleashing the Explosive Power of Your Mind to Maximize Health, Happiness, and Spiritual Well-Being
Super Genes: Unlock the Astonishing Power of Your DNA for Optimum Health and Well-Being

Serena Dyer and Wayne Dyer
Don't Die with Your Music Still in You: My Experience Growing Up with Spiritual Parents

Wayne Dyer
Change Your Thoughts, Change Your Life: Living the Wisdom of the Tao
I Can See Clearly Now
The Power of Intention

Louise Hay
Heal Your Body
The Power Is Within You
You Can Heal Your Life

Mahatma Gandhi and Richard Attenborough
The Words of Gandhi

Arianna Huffington
The following is the source of the William James quote in chapter 2 and also a look at how stress and burnout can get in the way of us truly thriving.
Thrive: The Third Metric to Redefining Success and Creating a Life of Well-Being, Wisdom, and Wonder

Nancy Levin
Jump ... And Your Life Will Appear: An Inch-by-Inch Guide to Making a Major Change

Barb Schmidt
The Practice: Simple Tools for Managing Stress, Finding Inner Peace, and Uncovering Happiness

Daniel J. Siegel, M.D.
Mindsight: The New Science of Personal Transformation

David Simon
Free To Love, Free To Heal: Heal Your Body by Healing Your Emotions

Tara Stiles
Slim Calm Sexy Yoga: 210 Proven Yoga Moves for Mind/Body Bliss

Eckhart Tolle
The Power of NOW: A Guide to Spiritual Enlightenment

Marianne Williamson
A Return to Love: Reflections on the Principles of "A Course in Miracles"

Online and Social Media

If you find that the works of any of the authors I included in the list above resonate with you, then check out their websites or social media. Many of them can be followed on Twitter or Facebook or have weekly email newsletters you can sign up for. Many also have YouTube channels with video content that will further inform and inspire. In addition, you can check out the following sites, which include sources referenced in this book as well as additional sources of inspiration:

chopra.com

This is the website for the Chopra Center, founded by Deepak Chopra and David Simon, where I did much of my initial learning about meditation and the mind-body connection. They offer a host of programs and classes at the Center and online, as well as free content in the way of articles, newsletters, and even recipes for healthier living.

ifm.org

The website for The Institute for Functional Medicine can help you learn more about this individualized, patient-centered approach to medicine. It can also help you find a physician in your area who not only looks at what is affecting your health, but how and why it occurred in the first place.

greatergood.berkeley.edu

The Greater Good Science Center at the University of California, Berkeley, has as their stated purpose to study "the psychology, sociology, and neuroscience of well-being, and teach skills that foster a thriving, resilient, and compassionate society." Their site offers a host of articles and other resources on subjects like gratitude, mindfulness, and happiness.

randomactsofkindness.org

The Random Acts of Kindness Foundation is a non-profit foundation that believes in the power of kindness to change the world. Its website and programs help spread kindness throughout schools and communities.

ted.com

TED is an organization dedicated to spreading ideas, typically in the form of short talks given by people from all walks of life, including many of the authors recommended above. You can watch free videos of these talks on their website, including one by Brené Brown on the Power of Vulnerability (ted.com/talks/brene_brown_on_vulnerability) that is almost sure to inspire.

thnx4.org

Offered by the Greater Good Science Center, thnx4.org is an online program for creating an interactive, shareable gratitude journal. Designed by experts in the field, it's a two-week program that will help you learn how to make gratitude a daily practice.

Apps

Conscious Health

Created by Deepak Chopra and the Chopra Center, this app provides a number of guided meditations by Chopra himself, which you can match with various music tracks to customize your own experience.

Fitbit

An app designed to help you lead a more active and healthier life, Fitbit tracks your health, exercise, and general activity level on a daily basis. It can help you get real insight into how much you're moving each day, how many calories you're burning, how much sleep you're getting, and so on, so you can make meaningful adjustments in your life that will enhance your overall well-being.

Insight Timer

This app helps you time your meditation sessions and connects you with a community of people around the world who also practice meditation. In addition, it offers guided meditations from some high-profile teachers like Eckhart Tolle, Jack Kornfield, and Thich Nhat Hanh.

Jiyo

This app is a well-being platform designed to help you lead a healthy lifestyle. It tracks your behavior and then offers information and suggestions on how to improve your habits. I use it mostly to track my personal health and fitness data, but it also covers other areas of your life, like relationships, finances, and even finding your purpose.

More Bliss Tools

Mini Meditations

When my students first start to practice meditation, many of them get frustrated quickly. They often say to me, "I can't get my brain to stop no matter how hard I try." My answer to them is always to stop trying. The purpose of Meditation is not to stop thinking, but to slow down our thoughts so we have a chance to choose the ones that serve us and let the others float away.

An easy way to practice this and work up to or supplement a regular mediation practice is to try what I call "mini meditations."

Mini Meditation #1:
Reset Yourself

When your computer freezes, what do you do? You hit the reset button to restart is. We can do something similar with our minds throughout the day. This exercise is especially useful if you find yourself getting worked up, overwhelmed, or stressed out. It's a quick and easy way to check yourself before you wreck yourself.

1) Any time you find the need to reset, find somewhere quiet where you can sit for 1 to 5 minutes.
2) Close eyes and focus on your breath.
3) Say quietly to yourself, "breathe in, breathe out, breathe in, breathe out."
4) Repeat this over and over until you feel your breath start to slow and your mind and body begins to calm.

Mini Meditation #2:
Tense Your Way Into Relaxation

This is a kind of body scan where you intentionally tense your muscles in order to get your body to relax. It sounds counter-intuitive but it works!

1) Start with the muscles in your toes and feat. Tighten them as much as you can. Hold for count of 5. Then release, relax, and let go.

2) Do the same with the muscles in your legs, holding for a count of 5, then releasing, relaxing, and letting go.
3) Continue in this way all the way up to the top of your body, ending with the muscles in your face.
4) When you've finishing, sit quietly for a moment and notice how your body feels. Compare it to how you felt before your started this mini mediation.

Mindful Self-Examination

Once I got a handle on meditating and was doing it regularly, I added another element to my daily practice. Now, when I sit down to meditate, I precede the meditation by asking myself a serious of questions. I don't force an answer; I just ask and see what comes to me. Once I'm done with these question, I start my regular meditation, only with these thoughts fresh in the back of my mind.

The questions are:

1) Who am I?
2) What do I want? What do I really, really want? What are my deepest desires? (The answer can be anything: material wants, career goals I want to reach, new habits I want to introduce into my life, spiritual or metaphysical desires—really, anything.)
3) What's my dharma or purpose in life? How can I help? How can I serve?
4) What am I grateful for?

Give Yourself a Strength Shower

I learned this exercise in the Creative Insight Journey course I took to become a transformational coach. It's a great way to see how others view you and also check in with your own thought patterns to see if you're viewing yourself clearly or if you're viewing yourself in a negative or limiting way. We can start to rewire our own thought patterns in this way and focus more on the positive.

You'll need a group of people to do this exercise, so if you have a group of friends you meet with regularly, a book club, or a class you're part of, enlist them to help. Each person in the group should prepare to tell a short story about themselves. It should be a story of success, of triumph, about a time in your life where you faced obstacles and you got past them. When I first did this exercise, I told the story of deciding, at the age of forty-nine, that I wanted to become certified to teach yoga. When I showed up for class the first day, I discovered I was one of the oldest people in the room. I immediately started having doubts, but instead of giving up, I set myself up to win. I set a goal of becoming certified before my fiftieth birthday and made a plan to help me reach it, enlisting the help of my daughter in the process. And it worked. I got certified and taught my first yoga class a full month before my fiftieth birthday.

Each person in the room will tell their own story of triumph, after which time the storyteller will just sit and listen—not responding, just taking it all in—as the others in the group point out the strengths they noticed in that person from the story that was told. For example, when I told my story, people said things like:

"Pam, the strength I see in you is that you're not afraid to try."
"Pam, the strength I see in you is that you know how to set yourself up for success."
"Pam, the strength I see in you is that you have perseverance."
"Pam, the strength I see in you is that you're brave."

This is what's called a "strengths shower." During it, one of the participants should be designated as the record keeper. She or he should write down all the strengths that people point out, and then give the list to the storyteller at the end of the session. It's very powerful to hear all the positive things that people think about you. They may even see things in you that you hadn't thought about before. It's even more powerful to walk away with a record of it all that you can refer to anytime limiting beliefs start to creep in.

A Sample Gratitude List

When you're making a gratitude list, try to expand your vision of what's worth being thankful for. The basics like family, friends, your work, your home, your good health, your pets, and the good healthy food you have to eat are a great place to start. But also think about what experiences you've had that you can be thankful for, like the great book you read recently, or the feeling of happiness you had that afternoon, or the old song you heard on the radio that had you singing out loud in your car and brought back old memories. You can even be thankful for your daily practice bringing you a sense of calm and peace on a regular basis.

After that, try pushing the idea of gratitude even further by asking yourself: What gratitude can I find in some of the more difficult or negative experiences I've had in my life? The answers could be things like:

I'm grateful for the tears that made me feel better.
I'm grateful for the fears that taught me a lesson about myself.
I'm grateful for the disappointments that lit a fire in me.
I'm grateful for the lost relationships that helped me see who I really am and what I really want in my life.

Sensory Gratitude Practice

In addition to simply asking yourself what you're grateful for on a daily basis, you can expand your sense of gratitude by considering the question through each of your five senses. Ask yourself:

What did I see today that I'm grateful for?
What did I hear today that I'm grateful for?
What did I smell today that I'm grateful for?
What did I touch or feel today that I'm grateful for?
What did I taste today that I'm grateful for?

The answers can be things like:

I'm grateful for the smiles I saw on people's faces.
I'm grateful for the laughter I heard today from my children.
I'm grateful for the smell of baking brownies that I experienced today when passing a bakery, which reminded me of my mom baking brownies for me as a child.
I'm grateful for the pat on the back from my supervisor who thought I did a great job.
I'm grateful for the delicious fruit I got at the farmer's market today. It tasted like summer!

Ideas for Committing Random Acts of Kindness

Random acts of kindness are meant to help, inspire, or enhance the day of someone for no particular reason other than because you want to. The Internet is full of examples of random acts of kindness, but if you need some ideas to get you started, consider the following. They are quick and easy enough that anyone can do them.

1) Give a gift at a random time. Who says gifts are just for holidays or birthdays? Why not give a gift just to tell someone how much you like or appreciate them? It doesn't have to be expensive or elaborate. In fact, something personal, like homemade food or flowers from your garden, makes a great gift that can be even more meaningful than something you purchase.
2) Write someone a note. This could be a card, a letter, or an email telling someone how important they are to you, what you like so much about them, or thanking them for something they've done for you recently. Be as specific as you can when you write the letter.
3) A kind gesture to a stranger. We encounter all sorts of people all day long, but unless we know them, we often barely acknowledge them, if we acknowledge them at all. You can really make someone's day by doing something unexpectedly nice for them instead, like holding open a door, letting them into traffic, letting them have the parking place you were about to take, or letting them go in front of you in line.
4) Offer up nonmaterial gifts as often as you can. There are a lot of things that can make someone's day that cost no

money at all and very little in the way of time or effort on your part. A smile can be given out easily and often to friends or strangers. A compliment can have a big impact, especially on someone who is having a tough day.

More Journaling for Self-Reflection and Discovery

As we learned in chapter 3, journaling is a great tool for processing your thoughts and feelings, helping you to set and attain goals, and for getting past difficult experiences in your life. In addition to the journal prompts I've already included in this book, you can use your journal as a space to really get to know and understand yourself, and to be more mindful and aware of who you are. Use the following prompts anytime you're unsure about what to write next.

Where Do I Come From?

Mining childhood memories is a great way to explore who you are and to consider how past experiences inform your choices and actions today.

What was I afraid of as a child?
What are some of my best childhood memories?
What did I love to do when I was young?
What were my favorite things (foods, books, toys, TV shows, etc.)?
Who were my best friends and why?
Who were my role models and why?

You can even get out some old photographs and use them to inspire your writing. Look at them and write down everything you remember about what was going on at that time, including:

How old was I?
Where was I?
Why was I in this place/doing this thing?
Who else was there?
What was I thinking at the time?
What was I feeling at the time?
What else was going on in my life at that time?

What Am I Afraid Of?

Think about the things that cause you fear today and spend some time exploring those fears in your journal through the following questions:

What am I afraid of?
When is the first time I remember feeling that fear? Describe the moment in as much detail as you can.
When was the last time I remember feeling that fear? Describe the moment in as much detail as you can.
Why do I think I'm afraid of this particular thing?
What have I been afraid of in the past that I no longer fear?
How did I get past that fear?

Relationships

A journal is a great place to process our thoughts and feelings about the people in our lives, past and present.

What relationships in my life have nurtured me the most? Why?

What relationship in my life is currently causing me the most struggle? Why?

Think about a relationship that was once important in your life but is no longer part of your life, then ask yourself:

What did I learn from being in that relationship?

What did I learn from the loss of that relationship?

What do I miss about the relationship?

What don't I miss?

Focus on the Positives

Too often, a journal becomes a place to dump only our bad, sad, angry, or frustrated feelings. Make an effort to record the positives as well, using the following prompts.

What am I great at?

What am I really passionate about?

What are my best qualities?

What brings me joy and happiness?

Think about some of your favorite things in life. These could be anything from food to music to people to experiences. Then spend some time describing them and what you like so much about them.

What was the best concert I've ever been to? (Describe it and what was so memorable about it.)

What are some of the best books I've ever read? (Describe them and what you loved about them.)

What was the best meal I've ever had? (Describe it and what was so memorable about it.)

What was the best day of my life? What happened on that day, and why was it so great?

What Matters Most in My Life?

Spend some time thinking about what is most important to you in your life. Then spend some time with your journal, describing those things and what's important to you about them. Write about what life would be like if you didn't have them. Some topics you might write about include:

your marriage/relationship
your children
your job/career
your home
your pets
your friend
your hobbies

Who Am I?

Fill in the blank with as many words or phrases as you can think of:

I am ____________

Once you've described yourself as fully as you can, ask some people close to you to describe you in words or phrases.

Record what those people say about you and then compare it to your description of yourself. Then ask yourself:

How does what I think about myself compare to what others think of me?

Where do our descriptions overlap?

Where do our descriptions differ?

How do I feel about how others described me?

How do I now feel about how I described myself?

Letter Writing 101

Instead of writing in your journal to no one in particular, pretend you are writing someone a letter. You don't need to ever send the letter to the person you're addressing, though you can if you chose to.

Write a letter to someone that you're angry at.

Write a letter to someone who has meant a lot to you but probably doesn't know it.

Write a letter to one of your role models or to someone you admire.

Write a letter to someone who has passed away or whom you have lost touch with.

Write a letter to your future self. What are your hopes and wishes for that person of tomorrow?

Write a letter to your past self. What would you want to say to the person you were back then?

Acknowledgments

It has taken me more than two years to envision, write, re-write, and finally get the courage to jump by letting this book out into the world. I would like to thank everyone who has inspired, encouraged, and supported me along the way. I couldn't have done it without the following wonderful group of people …

My daughter Brittany—I knew you were special from the moment you were born. You came into this world a fighter and have continued to show your courage, determination, and strength. You have a caring and compassionate heart, along with an abundance of spirit and enthusiasm for all that you do. May your dreams stay big and your worries stay small. I love you to the moon.

My mom and dad, Barbara and George, who taught me the values of hard work, perseverance, and determination and without whom none of this would have been possible.

My siblings and their spouses—Lynn and Dave, Bill and Ellen, Tom and Lisa—and my nieces and nephews—Tori, Whitney, Bradley, Andy, Betsy, Stuart, Peter, Walker—for being my sounding board and unfailing support system, and for just always having my back. To Bradley—I miss your loving spirit!

My ex-husband, Steve—for your willingness to fill in some of the pieces of my story, which was a great help in creating this book.

All my teachers and mentors who helped breathe life back into my being.

My other family at the Chopra Center and the Chopra Foundation, for your commitment to creating a peaceful, just, sustainable, healthy, and happier world, and for all the lessons you've taught me that I've been able to take and share with others.

Deepak Chopra, who put me on the path to healing and has continued to be a guiding light ever since.

Carolyn Rangel, for your friendship and guidance, as well as your thoughtful reading and advice on this manuscript.

Gabrielle Bernstein, my spiritual mentor, who helped me take a leap of faith and finally find the courage and confidence to write this book. You and your husband Zack, aka "Hollywood," have offered me a never-ending supply of encouragement, advice, and support; and to the alumni from Gabby's Spirit Junkie Masterclass, an amazing group of light leaders who are both inspiring and inspired.

Leon Nacson and the team at Hay House Publishing, as well as the crew at KN Literary Arts, including Kelly Notaras and Nikki Van De Car, for their publishing expertise.

Christa Bourg, for keeping me on task and for your patience, expertise, and writing and editing skills, which helped bring this book to life.

Barbara Schmidt, for your compassionate mentoring and for sharing your insights and experiences.

On my journey of spiritual growth and transformation, I began to hear the call to share what I've learned, inspire others, and help them connect to a greater purpose. My students have allowed me to fulfill this purpose and along the way, have taught me as much as I've been able to teach them—thank you to all of you!

About the Author

Pam Butler is a Certified Chopra Primordial Sound Meditation instructor, a certified yoga teacher, a Creative Insight Journey transformational coach, and a bliss coach who provides various workshops, classes, and one-on-one instruction to individuals, groups, and businesses throughout the South Florida community.

Pam's unique combination of body movement and mind practices comes from a place of deep experience. Grounded in mindfulness, her students safely explore ways to examine their individual responses to stress and learn specific techniques to shift into a state of balance and well-being. She creatively uses a mix of mediation, yoga, and other tools to help people:

- heal emotional anxiety
- create mental clarity and calmness
- increase body awareness

- relieve chronic stress patterns
- relax the mind
- center attention
- sharpen concentration

Pam also considers herself a lifelong learner and is always looking for ways to acquire new tools, insights, and inspirations that will help her, her students, and her listeners on their journeys. Most recently, she was invited by the Chopra Foundation to take part in their Self-Directed Biological Transformation Initiative (SBTI), the goal of which was to study how the practices of Ayurveda, meditation, and yoga can reverse biological markers of aging and alter cellular biology. This groundbreaking research study was done in collaboration with Harvard University; the University of California, San Francisco; Mount Sinai Hospital; Scripps Translational Science Institute; and the University of California, San Diego.

A native of Philadelphia, Pennsylvania, Butler resides in Fort Lauderdale, Florida.